Fly Fishing Mammoth

A Fly Fisher's Guide to the Mammoth Lakes Area

Mark J. Heskett

Frank Amato
PORTLAND

Dedication

To my wife Lori, who tolerates this mistress of mine called fly fishing. And to the memory of my late father-in-law Jim Palmer. If there's fishing in Heaven, he knows all the good holes.

Introduction

When I started fishing the Mammoth area over fifteen years ago, and being a neophyte fly fisher, I was starved for information. Unfortunately I could not find anything about fly fishing the area so I asked a lot of questions and kept a diary. There is no bigger information junkie than a fly fisherman. We collect, store and research more information than the F.B.I. We turn into book nerds and build extensive libraries. This is just part of the obsessive passion we call fly fishing.

Reflecting over the years, I felt the need to sit down and transfer this information to paper. When a person sits down to write a book, they are at the mercy of the reader. The audience you assume you are writing for is not always the mark you shoot at. I wrote this book with the intention that it be used. Throw it in the tackle bag or carry it in your vehicle on your fishing expeditions to the Mammoth area. Underline and write your observations in the margins. That's what I would do.

It is my hope to write the book I was looking for at the start of my journey, years ago. I trust that anglers who pick up *Fly Fishing Mammoth: A Fly Fisher's Guide to the Mammoth Lakes Area* will benefit from it. It is my aim to share with the fly angler information that will make the precious little free time we have on the water a more complete experience. If there is just one piece of information here that will help you as a fly fisher, I'll feel this journey was worth the

Published in 1994 by Frank Amato Publications, Inc.
P.O. Box 82112, Portland, Oregon 97282
ISBN: 1-878175-95-5
UPC: 0-66066-00187-0
Book Design: Charlie Clifford
Printed in Hong Kong
3 5 7 9 10 8 6 4 2

Contents

Part Three: Hatches and the Seasons .57

Part Four: Parting Thoughts 69

About the Author

Mark Heskett is a California native who has spent the last 16 years plying the waters of the Eastern Sierra with his fly rod. Mark's fly fishing obsession has taken him from Alaska to the Florida Keys and all points in between to cast flies at anything that swims.

He is a freelance writer and illustrator with credits in *Flyfishing* and *California Angler* and other fly fishing periodicals.

Mammoth Area Tackle Shops

Contact any of the shops listed below and they will give you the latest information about fishing conditions and hatches:

The Trout Fitter
P.O. Box 7026
Mammoth Lakes, CA 93546
(619) 924-3676

The Trout Fly
P.O. Box 407
Mammoth Lakes, CA 93546
(619) 934-2517

Sierra Bright Dot
(Guide Service)
(619) 934-5514

Kittridge Sports
(619) 934-7566

Rick's Sports Center
P.O. Box 3123
Mammoth Lakes, CA 93546
(619) 934-3416

Bibliography

Aquatic Insects of California, Edited by Robert L. Unsinger: University of California Press, 1963.
American Nymph Fly Tying Manual, Randall Kaufmann: Frank Amato Publications, Inc., 1975.
Complete Book of Fly Tying, The, Eric Leiser: Alfred A. Knopf, 1977.
Designing Trout Flies, Gary Borger: Tomorrow River Press, 1991.
Eastern Sierra, A Visitors Guide, Sue Irwin: Cachuma Press, 1991.
Fly Fisherman, July 1993, "Bead Heads," Tom Rosenbauer.
Mammoth Lakes Sierra, Rinehart, Dean, Elden Vestal, Betty E. Willard: Genny Smith Books, 1989.
Mighty Sierra, The, Paul Webster: American West Publishing Company, 1972.
Modern Fly Dressing for the Practical Angler, Poul Jorgensen: New Century Publishers, Inc., 1976.
Popular Fly Patterns, Terry Hellekson: Peregrine Smith, Inc., 1977.
Trout, Earnest Schwiebert: E. P. Dutton, 1978.
Western Trout Fly Tying Manual, Volume 1 and 2, Jack Dennis: Snake River Books, 1974, 1980.

Part One: Fishing Mammoth

Mammoth Lakes Area and History

There is a blacktop ribbon that winds through the eastern side of the Sierra Nevada mountain range called Highway 395. As it cuts its way between Ridgecrest and Bridgeport, six hours out of Los Angeles, it crosses another highway, 203. Three miles down this road and 7,800 feet above sea level, lays the town of Mammoth Lakes. The town is located in a glacial valley carved out eons ago and seated at the base of an old, worn volcano best known for its snow skiing. Over the centuries, water and ice have cut deep gashed canyons that surround the area. Jeffrey pine forests jut from the gray sierra granite, defiant survivors of the harsh winters that can produce an average 335 inches of snowfall a year.

Mention the name Mammoth Lakes at a cocktail party and most comments would be about the great skiing and winter sports the area offers. But mention the name in a group of fly fishers and names like Green Banks, Long Ears and Hot Creek Caddis hatches will pepper the conversation.

If you were to look for Mammoth Lake, you would not find it. Mammoth Lakes owes its name to a short lived mining town called Mammoth City that struggled between 1878-1879. It's possible these prospectors were the first to introduce rainbow trout into the area. It was common practice then to pack trout in milk cans for miles, strapped to a mule's back, and dump them in barren lakes.

It wasn't until 1928 that freight and passenger service by dog sled found a few hearty souls living year-round in Mammoth. In 1941 Dave McCoy installed the first rope tow on the mountain and that was the beginning of the ski resort. The area known for its trout fishing in the 1930s and 40s succumbed to skiing.

If the old-timers could see their boomtown now they would be slack jawed in amazement. Replacing the horses and oar carts are upscale four wheel drive vehicles, with brightly colored float tubes strapped on top, piloted by anglers traversing the town. These anglers are trying to catch the hatch on Hot Creek or possibly they heard about the damsel fly migration going on in the upper lakes. The renaissance of fly fishing has found Mammoth going full circle and the town best known for its winter sports is becoming a fly fishing town.

There is much to offer the fly fisher. From pack-in alpine lakes and boulder hopping streams that wind their way down volcanic rock, to rivers that meander through treeless meadows. Their under-cut banks hiding alert trout, waiting for the next meal to float by. There are pay-to-play ranches that offer some of the best dry fly fishing to be found.

Whether you are the hard core, match-the-hatch fly fisherman, a wife and kids family fly fisherman or anything between, you can find it here.

Equipment
Rods

Just as fiberglass replaced bamboo, graphite has done the same to fiberglass. The introduction of this space age material to rod building has given us a wide choice when it comes to picking a rod. A stroll through the aisle at your local fly shop will leave you per-plexed. There are high modulus, low modulus, lighter and thinner rods. Every year there is a breakthrough in rod design that threatens to date our high-priced rods. These are real changes in the world of rod building, not some ad man's idea to sell more rods.

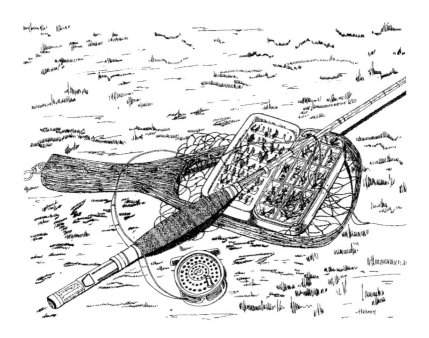

The popularity of fly fishing has created a highly competitive market beckoning for your hard earned bucks. This has benefited the angler immensely. Rod design has matured more in the last fifteen years than it has in the previous fifty. Don't worry, your costly graphite rod will not become outmoded that quickly. These year to year changes are subtle. My favorite five weight rod is nine years old and it still looks and casts like the current models.

An old heresy about rod length is use a long rod for big water and a short one for small water. This no longer is the case. Now we are seeing longer, lighter line weight rods used in most trout fishing. According to Tom Rosenbauer at Orvis, they see the trend going away from the old standby eight foot, six weight to an eight and a half to nine foot for five weight. The people at Sage also claim their most popular trout rod is nine foot for five weight. The new materials are enabling the rod builders to create lighter (in weight) but stronger rods.

This holds true when it comes to picking a rod for Sierra fishing. The most prevalent rod is the nine foot, five weight. The biggest benefit to the new stronger, lighter rods is not the ability to cast farther, it's that they help you combat the worst element that confronts the fly caster. Wind. You are going to confront this factor often. Count on it. Very seldom, if at all, will you find the need for a seventy foot cast. But you will find the need for accuracy on some waters that you fish.

If I could only have one rod for Sierra fishing it would be a nine foot for a five weight. If I were to pick two, the second would be a nine foot, three weight for some of the skinnier water that seems to hold the more nervous trout. I would spool this with a four weight fly line. Most casting with this rod will be between twenty and thirty feet and the heavier line loads the rod quickly on shorter casts.

Reels

Reels on the market now are victims of the same circumstance that rods fall into; their design has also benefited from the increased popularity of fly fishing. In the old days you just had Pfluger or Hardy reels to pick from. Now some trout reels are suffering from high-tech overkill. Just look at all the possibilities you have to pick from. I think a mega buck, cork drag reel is a bit much for a three-pound trout. If you stick with the simple click drag reel you are better off. Not only in your pocket book but you will have a basic functional, no hassle reel. A reel is subject to many harsh elements, such as blowing dust, grit and water. They get dropped on rocks and freeze on cold fall mornings. The fewer moving parts subjected to these elements, the better off you are. Don't get me wrong, I'm not saying these expensive reels are not worth the money. They are meticulously-machined works of art and if you find yourself flush with money, be my guest. In my opinion spend the money on a saltwater reel, one of these brutes will put a real workout on these sophisticated drag systems.

Look for a reel machined from bar stock for strength. The Orvis CFO is a good reel and their design permits quick spool changes without the fly line pinching in the frame. This brings up another thing to consider, along with your reel you need spare spools. You don't want to limit yourself to one fly line. One or two spare spools loaded with different line enables you to fish as the conditions demand. It also allows you to swap the reel to different weight rods.

Fly Lines

If you limit yourself to one fly line, you also limit your fishing. Use a floating line only and you are held to dry fly and shallow water nymphing most of the time. There are some exceptions but this is mostly the rule. The other two lines that are useful are the twenty foot, type 2 or 3 sink-tip, and a full sink line. These should be loaded on spare spools and carried in an easily accessible pocket in your vest.

The sink-tip is needed for fishing weed beds and nymphing when you want the fly to bounce along the bottom. It's also the line used for most fishing from a float tube. While the sink-tip portion of the line fills the bill for many situations, the floating portion of the fly line makes it more manageable than a full sinker.

Full sink line is the best choice when fish are hugging the bottom. Use full sink line with cold water conditions found in early spring or at midday when the bright sun forces trout into deeper water. Some anglers use this line for nymph fishing. The late Charlie Brooks was an advocate of nymphing with full sink line. Jim Teeny makes a T series sinking line that comes in different weights. These are marvelous lines with a uniform sink rate that eliminates the belly first sink rate that plagues some fly lines.

Using the proper fly line is one of the most overlooked areas in the angler's tackle. Often I have seen fly rodders using a floating line when they should be using a sink-tip or full sinker to get down to the fish. Using the right fly line is just as important as selecting the right fly pattern. Presenting the fly to the fish at its plane increases your chances of getting a strike.

There are a number of other fly line combinations and a shooting head system. The advantages of these items are that they allow you to use just one spool on your reel and change shooting heads as needed.

I think you will find that floating, sink-tip and full sinker will get you through most of your Sierra fly fishing situations. Stay away from fluorescent lines, buy olive or brown shades.

Most anglers prefer fly line in weight forward. They cast easier, farther and are more forgiving to the novice. The only advantage for the double taper over the weight forward would be in the lighter rods. It is at times that you are throwing dries with your three weight to spooky trout where the delicate presentation of lighter double taper is needed.

Leaders

Developments in leader materials have led to thinner leaders testing at the same strength as their older counterparts. I find no reason to be fishing lighter than 4X in the lakes. There are times you need to go heavier, such as in fall when the hogs come out to play.

With the new stronger materials you find in dry fly fishing you can go to a 7X with confidence on the harder fished waters. Situations present themselves where tippet sizes are important. Dry fly leaders can be between eight and eighteen feet, depending on the conditions. With wet fly leaders, there is no need to be longer than eight feet. Later in the season when weed beds become more abundant in the lakes you will want to use pretapered, knotless leaders. The absence of knots prevents the leader from picking up debris. Always keep your leader material stored in a vest pocket, out of the sun.

There are times when nymphing you will want to get some weight on the leader, I like to use size B split shot and add a strike indicator.

Vests

Since 1933 when Lee Wulff sewed the first vest, little has changed. I guess it's hard to improve on a good design. A good vest should have enough pockets to store fly boxes and other accessories, such as polarized glasses and other essentials that make your time on the water more pleasurable. Also make sure you have a couple of easily accessible pockets designed to store spare spools.

You might also consider a short vest for float tubing or any deep water wading you may do. Your vest should fit loose enough to allow freedom of movement when wearing a sweater or light jacket.

Waders

Neoprene waders have many advantages over nylon. Neoprenes stretch when you take a high step onto a stream bank and they insulate better, keeping you more comfortable when float tubing. You can also roll them down to your waist on hot days while stream fishing. On the other hand they are more expensive than nylon waders.

Nylon has its advantages as far as light weight and price. You can always don a pair of thin, silk long johns underneath them to keep you warm while float tubing.

Pick up a pair of neoprene booties like skin divers wear. These save wear and tear on the bottoms of your expensive waders as you walk down to the lake from your car.

Wading Boots

If you have a pair of boot foot waders you can skip this section and go on to the next. If not, read on. You will need a good pair of wading boots for any wade fishing you will be doing. You can always go the cheap route and get a pair of old tennis shoes to wear over your stocking foot waders. I wouldn't recommend this system. The bottoms are not well-suited to wading and they allow sand and gravel to invade them, chaffing your waders. Besides they look funky. What you want is a good pair of lace up boots with a felt bottom. Stay away from the velcro strap lace up system, they come loose in fast currents, which allows for a loose fit and debris into the boot.

Float Tubes

Your float tube is something you are going to spend hours of angling time in, so there are a few things you should look for. Make sure it has a good, high back rest, this will keep the water off you when paddling in choppy, windy conditions. (Note: If there is a breeze blowing and you think it is going to get a little choppy, put on your rain jacket. This will help keep you dry.) The backside of your tube should be a high visibility orange to make you easier to spot by the boats on the water. It should have a stripping apron and storage pockets. A fleece patch is also good and D rings make it convenient for clipping on your net. Some tubes also come with them on the bottom, allowing you to clip on a couple of straps so you can pack it on your back to those hike-in areas.

Accessories

Following are a few small things you need on the water to make your angling life easier:

Polarized glasses to cut the glare and make fish spotting easy. Always carry a stream thermometer, water temperature triggers activity in fish and insects. Knowing the water temperature helps you decide what the fish are doing. In extremely cold water (48 degrees or less) they slow and feed less. The same holds true for warm water (70 degrees or more). Trout become sluggish and hold in oxygenated water, such as riffles and runs.

If you tie your own flies, put together a portable kit. A friend of mine uses a tackle box to store a few materials, spare vice and tools. I carry a small travel tying case by Umpqua that holds a vice and tools and store my materials in a small nylon case that has individual ziplock bags inside for storing material. It's called a book worm and works quite well for storing materials and hooks.

Forceps, these are great for removing hooks or smashing down barbs; I clip a pair to a retractable zinger pinned to my vest.

Another slick item is the rod carrying case by Mountain Trader or DB Dunn. These cases allow you to pack your rod around set up and ready to fish, all you have to do is unzip the case, remove the rod and put it together. They also come in double rod models so you can carry a couple of fully-rigged rods.

Other things to remember: sun screen, insect repellent, raincoat and a small flashlight for your vest. This is just a general list— you will expand on it as you find other things you can't live without.

The Quarry

Trout of the Mammoth Lakes Area

Rainbow Trout - *Salmo gairdneri*

God bless the rainbow. They are closest to the fly fisher's heart. While the wily brown is considered the prize trout by some anglers, it is the airborne acrobatics of rainbow trout that gets the heart beating as if you had just spotted a traffic cop in the rearview mirror. Not native to the eastern slope of the Sierra, it is believed by

some that the early prospectors were the first to introduce rainbows into the area.

California rainbows have been introduced worldwide. Easily raised, this makes them the favorite fish of hatcheries. The famous 'bows of New Zealand come from the eggs of Sonoma Creek steelhead. When first introduced to many waters they seemed to vanish when they reached maturity. This was because the adults, overcome with their genetic urge to migrate to the sea, would make a run for the salt. It was discovered that the Kern and McCloud variations didn't exhibit this urge. This characteristic made them a preferred rainbow stock.

Many hybrid species of rainbows are also introduced into the waters of the Sierra. The Fish and Game have been experimenting in the last few years trying to find a hybrid that will grow to double-digit size in Crowley Lake.

Rainbows are planted more often in Sierra waters than all other trout species combined. The truck-supplied and airplane-dropped trout of now-a-days is very different from the milk can-planted trout of yesteryear.

Three distinct strains of rainbow are introduced into the Mammoth Lake area. The Fish and Game feel the various strains of trout are necessary because they spawn at different times, allowing Fish and Game to stock all season long to meet its seasonal requirements.

The first is the Kamloops. This trout is best known for its aerial antics. A hooked Kamloops will tear up the surface of the water in repeated jumps, trying to regain its freedom. This is the sight that conjures up memories of old sporting magazine covers; airborne, red-slashed, slab sided rainbows trying to break free, the fly embedded in its jaw. A gossamer-thin thread of tippet is the only thing that separates the angler from becoming a hero or a Homer.

Coleman rainbows are next in the trio. They're popular with anglers because of their stubborn head-shaking fighting ability. They are a steelhead strain from the Shasta-Mount Lassen area. This fish exhibits good growth potential and does quite well in Crowley Lake. They are raised in the Hot Creek hatchery and the eggs sold to the Alper's River Ranch. Here they are pampered on a rich diet and reared to the incredible sizes of five to ten pound fish in three years. These are in turn sold to Mono County for stocking the area waters.

Eagle Lake are the third strain of rainbow common to the area. They make up many of the rainbows you get into in the fall. This distinctive species when stocked into the lakes seems to take on silver hues and a blue-green back.

Brown Trout - *Salmo trutta*

Brown trout eggs were first brought to this country crated in iced-down moss from Germany in 1883. They were planted in Sierra lakes and streams in 1895. The California state record is 26-pounds,

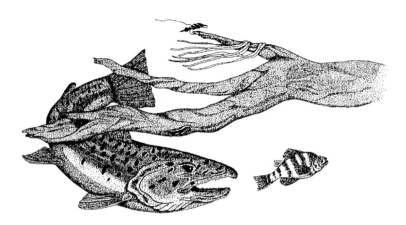

eight ounces.

Get a group of anglers together and Mr. Brown is always a subject of lively conversation, considered the Holy Grail of trout by some anglers and the freshwater great white by others. The majority will be enthusiastic about the cunning elusiveness of this sport fish. They talk about the great weight it grows to and how hard it is to dupe a big one to the fly. But there is a small camp of anglers that tell you the reason for this is the cannibalistic nature of the brown. While they are growing to these great sizes the other trout populations are paying the price. The fact is browns do outeat other trout for the simple reason that they outgrow and outlive other trout in our relentlessly fished waters. This is due to the elusive nature of the brown and their being nocturnal feeders.

Once they reach around sixteen inches they become meat eaters. You regularly hear stories about big browns caught with their stomachs containing mice or even a couple of baby ducks. It seems every season the Mammoth area kicks out a few of these big meat eaters in the double-digit size, more than once by some little kid soaking salmon eggs with a department store-bought Zebco, spooled with last years curly-cued monofilament. Ouch.

No matter how you feel about the brown you have to agree that one of the most beautiful sights is a hook jawed male in his fall colors.

Eastern Brook Trout - *Salvelinus fontinalis*
When you think of the square tail, visions of tree shaded alpine streams come to you, the trout of the Currier & Ives prints.

The smell of the sweet pine-needle carpet, is thick in the crisp mountain air. Cool mountain water dances over the river smooth boulders, forming pools that hold the brightly colored brookies.

Introduced to California in 1872 the eastern brookie is a char, not a true trout. The California state record is nine-pounds, 12 ounces. The strain that inhabits the Sierra was developed by Seth Green in the late 1800s. He experimented with an artificial strain that would mature earlier and spawn when they reached the size of six to eight inches. To this day, this genetic flaw is carried in the stocks of brookies across the nation.

Though most brookies in the fist-rate waters of the Sierra are small, Kirmin Lake in the Bridgeport area does hold brook trout in the four pound class. Brookies have the reputation of being gullible and easier to fool than brown and rainbow in the same water. Their bright color makes them easier to spot in the water when they rise to a dry fly and brookies are excellent for the angler who likes to fish dries on light tackle.

The best brook trout water in the Mammoth area has to be the basin lakes. In fall the upper Twin gives up some beautifully colored fish, the males displaying bright orange bellies with the fins richly painted in the same color. The leading edges of the lower fins are snow white and there are worm-like markings on the dark green back. The sides are marked with red and gray spots, surrounded in blue halos. At this time of year the fish are aggressive, striking hard at any fly that crosses their path.

The disadvantage to brook trout is that they will take over a fishery. When introduced to an area they rapidly outbreed the competing species in the area. They have occasionally done irreversible harm to some native species. Even with this downfall they provide welcome sport for the Sierra angler.

Cutthroat Trout - *Salmo clarki henshawi*

This trout has been native to the Sierra waters since Fred Flintstone's time. This is a strain of cutthroat that comes from watersheds that drained into prehistoric Lahontan Lake. The watershed covered most of Nevada and parts of California in the Pleistocene times, today only Pyramid and Walker Lakes remain today. Lahontan cutts were nearly decimated in the late 1800s and early 1900s by early miners and pioneers. Pyramid Lake holds the dark honor as being one of the world's most commercially exploited freshwater fisheries. Thousands of spawning cutthroats were netted from its waters.

The California state record is 31-pounds, eight ounces. The strains of cutthroat now in Mammoth waters are from Lake Heenan brood stock lake in Alpine County. Eggs from Heenan Lake breeders are distributed to the Hot Creek and McCloud hatcheries, they are then introduced into the area lakes and streams.

Cutthroats are closely related to rainbows and have a tendency to breed with them in the waters they are introduced into. Many waters in the west hold populations of cuttbows. Although the cutthroat is not known among anglers for its fighting abilities, this hybrid puts up a tenacious fight and doesn't surrender easily to the angler.

The cutthroat thrives in eastern Sierra alkaline rich water. The downfall of the cutt is that it is easily deceived by the fly, this makes them readily over-harvested. This has brought restricted methods of take in some of the more famed cutthroat water.

Golden Trout - *Salmo aguabonita*

The golden trout is the state fish of California. The state record is a whopping nine pound, eight ounce trout. If you have fished for any of these high mountain beauties you know what I mean, a two pound golden is considered a trophy to the backpack and granola crowd. These are not roadside fish in the Sierra, if you want to fish for them you have to work for them. The golden lives in elevations higher than 6,800 feet. The distribution area of the golden is limited, this means a walk. The best spot to find these fish in the Mammoth area is Laurel Lake.

The coloration of the golden makes it one of the most beautiful trout of the Sierra. It is the only species of *salmonidae* which retains its parr marks throughout its life. The tail and most of the body are a golden yellow color covered with large black dots. The dorsal, anal and ventral fins are usually white-tipped. One theory about the golden's coloration is that it evolved to protect it from harmful solar radiation that occurs at higher elevations.

There are currently two subspecies of goldens recognized in California. The South Fork Kern golden, native to the upper portions of the South Fork Kern River and Golden Trout Creek. The other is the Little Kern golden trout from the Little Kern River and its tributaries. In 1978 this species was listed as threatened by the U.S. Fish and Wildlife Service. Since then an aggressive management plan was implemented jointly by the Department of Fish and Game, the Fish and Wildlife Service, the Forest Service and the National Wildlife Service. Imagine trying to get all these bureaucrats together to formulate a plan. Whew!

The resulting plan calls for extensive habitat restoration and chemical eradication of all nonnative trout in lakes and streams that have been determined golden trout water. Pure strain goldens are then restocked. Certain brood stock lakes have also been set aside for the sole purpose of egg production. These produce the fingerlings for the planting of these waters.

The golden has excellent fighting qualities and is even considered equal to the rainbow by some anglers. It takes the fly eagerly but is not as vulnerable as the brookie and cutthroat.

Flies

The Ten Best and How to Tie Them

The following is a list of ten patterns that are indispensable to the Sierra fly fisher. These are scarcely the only flies you need—they

are the basics for you to build around. The more you fish the Mammoth area, the more familiar you become with specific hatches. Then you can fine-tune your fly box with specific patterns.

As I look through my fly boxes I find a pattern for just about every stage of the life cycle for the native aquatic insects. There is also a good mixture of terrestrial patterns. You can possess too many flies, and there are a few in there I have never used but I can't get rid of them—you never know!

There are also certain patterns that you will be tying regularly if you fish the Mammoth Lakes area repeatedly. Following are the flies that keep you attached to the chair at your tying bench.

Matuka

This pattern has spent more time underwater in the Sierras than a German U boat in the North Atlantic. The Matuka is the number one trout snagger in Crowley Lake.

Originally from New Zealand, the success of this fly is in the fact that it simulates many things in the aquatic world. This pattern gets more customized by the Crowley Lake regulars than some teenagers' first cars. There are many variations and it seems like when someone uses a new material in the recipe they feel it warrants a new name. What they have is a Matuka with an unconventional twist, not Joe's Sierra Fish Killer Special.

The most popular is the Olive Matuka. This resembles the perch fry that inhabit Crowley Lake. I believe it also resembles a damselfly nymph in other lakes. Other colors that are effective in Crowley are purple and yellow, and this pattern tied with a mylar body is also enticing to trout. (Note: When using a Mylar body, an olive floss underbody is tied first). The additional flash of the mylar body is the attraction in the algae-stained waters of the lake.

This pattern is most effective in summer and fall when the aquatic life they imitate is most abundant. The most exciting way to fish the Matuka is around weed beds, trout like to hide in them waiting for an easy meal to swim by. A Matuka cast into these feeding lanes on a sink-tip line provokes trout to strike.

The uniqueness of the Matuka style is the wing tied to the body with tinsel ribbing. This prevents the wing from becoming fouled around the hook when casting, like in other streamer patterns. Following is the recipe for the Olive Matuka.

Thread: *Black monocord*
Hook: *Mustad 9672*
Sizes: *4-10*
Underbody: *Lead wire*
Body: *Olive Hare-Tron Dubbing. (or Mylar, see note)*
Tail and Wing: *Olive dyed grizzly*
Ribbing: *Gold oval tinsel*
Throat: *4 or 5 wraps of red floss*
Collar: *Olive dyed grizzly*

Woolly Bugger

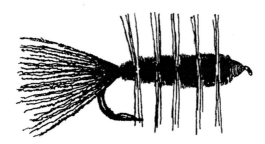

If ever there was a one fly contest in the Mammoth Lakes area, the Woolly Bugger would be the fly to use. It is one of the most versatile subsurface patterns around. What makes it so successful is the undulating action of the fly created by tying the lead on the forward shank of the hook. Using a soft hen hackle gives the fly a pulsating action, this combined with a marabou tail gives the fly a lively presentation that trout find irresistible.

By changing the color they imitate many things, such as leeches and damselfly nymphs. The olive color in size eight and ten is successful in the basin lakes such as Twin and Mary during the damselfly migration. Cast around the weed beds on a sink-tip line to produce the kind of wide open fishing you will not forget for a while. The purple, brown or black colors work well in the larger sizes in Crowley Lake. Another technique that works is to creep a Woolly Bugger along the bottom on a full sink line, this can be productive at times when nothing else works.

I know anglers who swear by this method on Hot Creek, when cast to the other shore and ripped across the current it drives the browns wild. I find this a little amusing, being productive on water that is so well known for requiring precise presentations and classic dry fly fishing.

Thread: *Black monocord*
Hook: *Mustad 9672*
Sizes: *4-12*
Tail: *Black marabou*
Underbody: *Lead wire (wrapped over the first third of the shank)*
Body: *Green, black, brown or purple. Peacock herl is also effective*
Ribbing: *Blue dun neck or saddle palmered over body. (When tying a purple Woolly Bugger use all purple in the pattern)*

Pheasant Tail Nymph

This pattern was developed by Frank Sawyers. A proper English gentleman whose patterns reflect the philosophy of simple, yet effective. The Pheasant Tail Nymph has become a classic pattern that is useful on all the trout waters that you will fish. The secret of this pattern is the slim silhouette that resembles many mayfly nymphs found in the Sierra waters. Add the fact it is a simple to tie nymph pattern and will not take up much of your time at the vice to fill your fly box. This is a blessing. As effective as this pattern is, you will be constantly refilling your fly box.

The Pheasant Tail is an absolute must on Hot Creek, where the weed beds offer great hiding places for the trout. They will hold there, invisible, only exposing themselves for a quick, easy meal as it floats by. That is the time this pattern is deadly fished with a strike indicator over the weeds.

Thread: *6/0 prewaxed tan*
Hook: *Mustad 3906B*
Sizes: *10-14*
Tail: *Pheasant tail fibers*
Ribbing: *.005" diameter copper wire*
Body: *Pheasant tail fibers*
Wingcase: *Pheasant tail fibers*
Legs: *Pheasant tail fibers*
Thorax: *Peacock herl over layers of copper wire*

Gold Ribbed Hare's Ear

This pattern is to the nymph fisher what the Adams is to the dry fly fisher. It is an old wet fly pattern and can simulate many species of aquatic life. Like the Pheasant Tail, when tied in different hook sizes it covers a wide spectrum of mayflies that inhabit the waters of the Mammoth area.

Where the Pheasant Tail sports a streamlined, slim body the Hare's Ear differs. It is wrapped with some scruffy hare's mask body that looks like a fat juicy meal to the trout.

This fly works great around weed beds that appear in the lakes during summer and provide apartment buildings for *Callibaetis*. Cast along the edges and slowly strip back in a short retrieve, this simulates the nymphs as they dart in and out of the weeds. No matter how you fish this pattern it is a trout getter. Every serious fly fisher should have a collection of these in their fly box.

Thread: *Prewaxed brown*
Hook: *Mustad 3906B*
Sizes: *8-18*
Tail: *4 or 5 strands of woodduck flank*
Ribbing: *Fine oval gold tinsel*
Body: *Dubbed hare's ear*
Wingcase: *Mottled brown turkey*
Thorax: *Dubbed hare's ear, picked slightly with dubbing needle to suggest legs*

Adams

Among fly fishers there is a saying, "When in doubt, tie on an Adams." One of the most popular dry flies in the western states, the Adams has deceived more than its share of trout. The reason for the success of this pattern is that it simulates several natural streamborn insects. The muskrat gray body can also be substituted with other colored dubbing when you want to key in on specific hatches. I prefer to tie these in the smaller sizes 14, 16 and 18 and lightly hackle them. Most of the water in the Mammoth area is of the spring creek and lake type and the heavily hackled, fast water type flies are not needed.

This fly reminds me of a friend of mine. A few years ago he decided he wanted to learn to fly fish so I agreed to show him some of my favorite spots in the Sierra. This one morning found us on the East Walker at the time known for its big browns. It was a typical July morning with a mist rising off the water, concealing the river under its veil. I put him on my favorite pool, had him tie on a white marabou streamer and instructed him to fish it down and across. This method had produced some nice browns for me out of this pool in the past.

Leaving him there, I worked my way downstream. As the morning sun chased the mist off the water and warmed the air, a hatch of light colored mayflies started. I clipped off the streamer and knotted on a size 16 Adams. As the intensity of the hatch increased so did the trouts' interest. The surface of the pools were dimpling with rising fish and they nailed the Adams as I jumped pool to pool.

After a couple of hours I decided to start back and see how my rookie friend was doing.

Reaching the truck parked at streamside, I found my pal sitting on the tail gate. He appeared as if he had just undergone an IRS audit.

"How's the fish?" I asked.

"No fish here, how about you?"

I went on to tell him how I had tagged the browns downstream on an Adams.

"Yeah, right."

As all this was going on, in the pool behind him a good fish was rising to the mayflies as they drifted past. Opening my fly box, I passed over an Adams and told him to try it in the pool behind him. Being a sport, he plucked the fly from my outstretched palm not even looking to the pool as he knotted the size 16 Adams on. Having no confidence in the fly it was apparent he was doing this to amuse me. Stepping into the pool, he false cast the fly and dropped it right on the nose of the trout. He had no idea the fat brown was there. An instant later the surface exploded in a crown shaped splash. The trout feeling the sting of the hook went aerial. Catching my unsuspecting friend off guard, he reared back on the airborne fish, the trout popped the overstretched tippet like sewing thread. It was over as fast as it started. Observing this split second lesson from my streamside perch, I watched in amusement at my denied friend as he pivoted in the pool to face me.

"Got another Adams?"

Thread: *Prewaxed black*
Hook: *Mustad 94845*
Sizes: *12-20*
Tail: *Dark moose hair, or mixed brown and grizzly hackle fibers*
Body: *Dubbed gray muskrat fur*
Wing: *Grizzly hackle tips*
Hackle: *Mixed grizzly and brown*

Olive Parachute

The two most common mayflies in the Mammoth Lakes areas are the *Ephemerella*, or Pale Morning dun, and the *Baetis*, better known as the Blue-Winged Olive. The Olive Parachute tied in different sizes is used successfully on both hatches. The parachute hackle allows the fly to float low on the water, presenting a realistic silhouette on slow-moving spring creeks such as Hot Creek. The deer hair wing catching the sunlight gives it a smoky appearance, simulating the natural as it floats downstream, riding the currents. *Baetis* is an early spring and late summer emerger, usually presenting itself in May and early June and then again in August. The *Ephemerella* is a midseason emerger, usually presenting itself in late June and early July. This pattern tied in various sizes (14-20) works well for you during these months. Note that this is a slow water pattern and will not fish well in early season run off conditions. It is unlikely though, that you will find a hatch of these mayflies going off in early spring run off conditions.

Thread: *Prewaxed olive*
Hook: *Mustad 94845*
Sizes: *14-20*
Tail: *Blue dun hackle*
Body: *Dubbed pale olive Hare-tron*
Wing: *Deer hair tied posted*
Hackle: *Blue dun wrapped parachute style*

Marabou Damsel Nymph

The damselfly is to the Sierra what the stonefly is to Montana. The Mammoth area lakes are so abundant with weed beds that when the damselfly migration goes on from late June through early August it produces remarkable fishing. There are days when it's too easy and tends to spoil an angler.

Damselflies are excellent swimmers. Of all aquatic emergers the damsel exibits the most action with its snake-like swim through the water. Over the years, fly tiers have come up with many patterns to imitate the *Odanata zygoptera* family but the undulating action of the marabou material seems to trigger a feeding response better than fur dubbed patterns.

I prefer to use peacock herl for the wingcase because this material seems to be such a great trout attractor. I also like to use plastic beads for the eyes. I don't know if this makes much of a difference to the trout but it does to me.

This is definitely a lake pattern and should be fished in a short jerky retrieve. Don't be afraid to experiment with your retrieve. This pattern is simple and effective and once you experience the great damselfly fishing still waters of Mammoth have to offer you will be hooked for life.

Thread: *6/0 olive*
Hook: *Mustad 9672*
Sizes: *8-12*
Tail: *Marabou barbs, same length as hook*
Body: *Marabou*
Wingcase: *Peacock herl*
Thorax: *Marabou, lightly plucked out with a dubbing needle to simulate legs*

Elk Hair Caddis

Al Troth, a Montana fly tier known for his practical creations, developed this successful pattern. It broadly simulates the variety of caddis hatches that occur in the Sierra waters. This is a buoyant, quick drying fly that is durable because of its elk hair wing and palmer hackled body. The tan colored wing makes the fly more visible, which is helpful in the smaller sizes. Although I feel the mayfly is the preferred diet of the trout, the caddis hatch is so prolific in the Sierra that trout feed on them with great abandon.

This pattern can be fished in the classic upstream cast or the wind can be used to present the fly downwind by skating it across the water's surface. This action imitates the natural as it bounces across the water, ovipositing its eggs in the stream. It can also be fished as a floating dropper when using a nymph.

Thread: *Prewaxed 6/0 tan*
Hook: *Mustad 94845*
Sizes: *12-18*
Body: *Hareline hare's ear dubbing*
Ribbing: *Fine gold wire*
Wing: *Cream colored elk flank hair*
Hackle: *Furnace or dark brown*

Royal Wulff

    This pattern is a take off on the classic Royal Coachman. It was developed as part of the Wulff series by the late Lee Wulff. By using a calf tail wing, it makes the fly more visible and durable.

    This pattern doesn't imitate any particular insect. It's an attractor pattern but there is just something about the thing that looks like a fat, juicy meal to the trout. It's an absolute killer on the San Joaquin River in Devil's Postpile. It's also effective on the back country lakes where brookies can't resist them.

    There are times you come across a selectively feeding fish that will turn up its nose at your match-the-hatch offering. Try the Royal Wulff. Sometimes you have to intrigue a selective fish by offering him something different. A few drag-free floats over his choosy head might turn up some surprising results.

Hook: *Mustad 94845*
Sizes: *10-20*
Thread: *Black monocord*

Tail: *Moose hair*
Wing: *Divided white calf tail tied upright*
Body: *Three to four wraps of peacock herl followed by red floss then three to four more wraps of peacock herl*
Hackle: *Brown neck*

Chamois Nymph

The caddisfly is one of the most abundant aquatic insects in the Mammoth Lakes area. Different species seem to hatch all season long. A good caddis nymph imitation will keep you on the fish. This pattern was shared with me by an old Sierra regular who swears by it and after using it on the Owens River I can see why he is so enthusiastic about it. When wet, the light chamois body is a good imitation of the *Rhyacophila* that is found in the area waters.

This pattern is best fished with a floating line, some split shot, and bounced along the bottom. A strike indicator helps in detecting strikes. It is most effective when fished in June-July, during the main part of the *Rhyacophila* emergence.

Hook: *Mustad 3906*
Sizes: *12-18*
Thread: *Black monocord*
Body: *1/8 inch strip of chamois wrapped and glued on #3 lead wrapped hook shank*
Thorax: *Black ostrich*
Beard Hackle: *A few turns of black hackle*

More Flies

The preceding list is for ten flies I feel you cannot be without in your fly box. The following is a more simplified list of other flies you will want to round out your selection.

Bead Head Flies

The last couple of years have found this pattern snowballing in

popularity among fly fishers. Across the states this is becoming the number one pattern with guides. A big part of its acceptance is because you can exclude the use of split shot to get the fly down. With the use of weight you are continuously experimenting with where to put it to get the right presentation.

Another reason for the success of bead head flies is in the sparkle of the head. Emerging insects develop a gas bubble between the exoskeleton and skin, creating a mirrorlike effect on the surface of the nymph. In short, the attraction of the flashy bead head seems to move fish. This fly sinks like a Danforth anchor, so there is no need to throw slack line or upstream mends.

Bead heads seem to work the best in fast current cobble bottom or rough gravel. In other words caddis water, which there is an abundance of in the Sierra.

Last, this is an environmentally safe fly. It eliminates the use of lead weight, thus leaving the stream cleaner when you don't leave the bottom cluttered with lead after losing a dozen flies after a days fishing.

The smallest bead available right now is a 1/8 inch that is just right for size 12 to 16 hooks. Looking at the bead you will notice it is drilled slightly larger at one end. You will want to slip the small end over a hook with a smashed down barb. Using a pair of forceps to grab the bead, twist the hook until the bead slips over the bend. Slide the bead up to the eye. Once you start to tie the pattern the thread and materials hold the bead in place. The two patterns you will find most useful are the Hare's Ear and Pheasant Tail. Below are two other variations you may want to try.

Bead Head Caddis
Hook: *Mustad 3906, Daiichi 1130 or Tiemco 2847*
Size: *12-16*
Thread: *Tan prewaxed 6/0*
Head: *Solid brass bead head 1/8" diameter*
Body: *Hare's ear or blend, colors to match the natural*

Bead Head Mayfly
Hook: 2XL or 3XL standard nymph hook
Size: 10-16
Thorax: Solid brass bead 1/8" diameter
Tail: Woodduck fibers
Rib: Copper wire rib
Abdomen: Olive or brown dubbing
Wingcase: Dark goose quill fibers
Legs: Brown Hungarian partridge fibers

Understanding Drag

With all this talk about bead head flies and adding split shot to the tippet, if you don't understand why we add lead to the fly this will not make sense. The surface speed of the stream is much quicker than the speed of the water over the bottom. This is a part of the science of hydraulics. This is why weight is added to the tippet or the fly—to slow it down to match the speed of the natural as it bounces along the bottom.

Still More Flies

Dry Flies

Hemmingway Caddis, sizes 18-12. CDC Caddis, 18-12. King's River Caddis, 18-12. Blue-Winged Olive, 20-22. Olive Comparadun, 20-22. Mosquito, 20-12. Griffith's and Black Gnat's, 20-18 (These are used on midge hatches). Trico CDC Spinners, 20-22 (Blue-Winged Olive spinner fall). Red Quill, 18-12

Nymphs

Peeking Caddis, 18-12. Biot Midge, 14-18. Biot Midge Emerger, 14-18. Brassy, 14-22. Bird's Nest, 14-18. Prince Nymph, 10-18. Zug Bug, 10-18 (These two patterns work as damselfly nymphs) Scud, 12-18. A. P. Nymph, 14-20. Tan San Juan Worm, 14. (Hot Creek)

Terrestrials

Dave's Hopper, Schroeder's Para-Hopper, 8-14. Deer Hair Beetle, 12-14. Dave's Cricket, 12-14. McMurry Ant, 14-20.

Part Two: The Area

Rivers and Streams of the Mammoth Range

Owens River

Whiskey is for drinking, waters for fighting over.
—**Mark Twain**

This saying fits the Owens River better than any other in California. Most rivers in the state flow to sea but the rivers of the eastern slope of the Sierra are an exception. If they are not piped into an aqueduct to nurture a thirsty Los Angeles, they course into a parched desert irrigating an occasional crop on the way.

Since the 1930s, a fight for the water rights on this river has been going on between the City of Los Angeles lawyers and the Sierra rancher. Called "Wakopee" by the Paiute Indians, Captain John Freemont named the river Owens after a leader of the 1845-46 expedition into the area. The river begins life as a spring creek flowing out of the eastern slopes in the area of Big Springs. The first three miles of river is open to the public for fishing. The river cuts a winding path through golden meadow pasture land and flows the next 10 miles across three private ranches. 10 to 12 miles later it dumps into Crowley Lake, the largest reservoir in the L.A. aqueduct system. At the end of the reservoir it flows through the Long Valley Dam on its way to the intake, south of Big Pine. Because the river is divided into two sections, I'll cover it in upper and lower portions.

Upper Owens River

The headwaters of the river start as a spring creek in the Big Springs area found on Owens River Road just off Highway 395 heading north toward June Lake. This is a typical California mountain stream, fast and brushy. As the river winds its way to Crowley Lake it passes through Alper's Owens River Ranch and the Arcularius Ranch. A Fish and Game electroshock survey in this section produced 11,047 fish per mile. 2,262 browns and 8,785 rain-

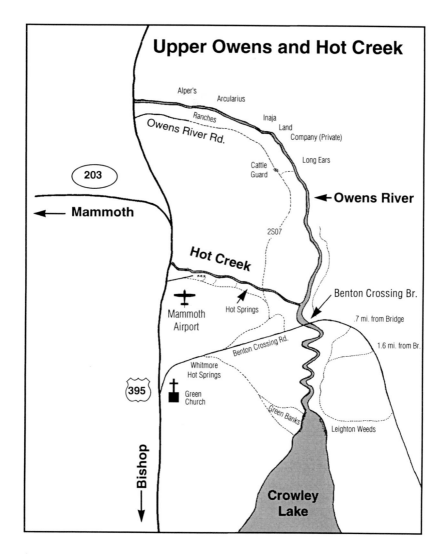

Upper Owens and Hot Creek

Alper's

Arcularius

Ranches

Owens River Rd.

Inaja
Land
Company (Private)

Long Ears

Cattle
Guard

203

◄— **Mammoth**

◄— **Owens River**

2S07

Hot Creek

Benton Crossing Br.

Mammoth
Airport

Hot Springs

.7 mi. from Bridge

1.6 mi. from Br.

Benton Crossing Rd.

Whitmore
Hot Springs

395

Green
Church

Green Banks

Leighton Weeds

Bishop

**Crowley
Lake**

bows. As it leaves private water the river slows to riffles and pools as it snakes through summer cattle pasture. Along its journey it carves deep, undercut banks which conceal wary trout. The upper section of river from the boundary of the L.A. Department of Water and Power land to the old Benton Crossing pilings downstream has been designated wild trout waters. There is a special regulation on this section all season—flies or artificial lures with barbless hooks, and a bag limit of two fish of 18 inches minimum.

During spring runoff, an off-color river flows rapidly making fly fishing hard for spring run Kamloops. Later in the season when water flows settle down, the river gives good hatches of Pale Morning Duns, caddis, damsels, and *Callibaetis*. Late summer, the river also produces good hopper fishing and a stonefly hatch. The character of the river in this stretch is winding meadow, absent of bushes or vegetation to hide the angler. Naturally, you should approach the river cautiously and quietly. Also with the absence of trees and bushes to form a wind break, the wind can become quite nasty in the afternoon.

The public portion of river includes the Big Springs area above Alper's Ranch. It continues at the old Long Ears Ranch that is now Department of Water and Power land below Inaja Land Company. You can follow the dirt road (2S07) on along a portion of the Owens before it dumps you onto the Benton Crossing Road. Go right and you'll head back to 395 below Mammoth Lakes. Go left and you head to Benton Crossing, above Crowley Lake. If you wish to bypass the Big Springs and Long Ears section, you can enter Benton Crossing Road off Highway 395 below Mammoth. The road is marked by Green Church at the intersection of the two roads. As you continue to the Benton Crossing Bridge you will pass two dirt roads to your right, just past Whitmore Hot Springs. These roads lead to the Green Banks and the north landing area of Crowley Lake. Passing over the bridge at Benton Crossing you will find Brown's Camp, a small campground with R.V. and tent sites and a modest general store. Although it is a private campground you can fish the river in this section as long as you check in with the general store and leave the license plate number of your vehicle.

If you continue to follow the road (2S84) to Crowley Lake, you will cross several dirt roads leading to the river on your right. Take the third one (1.6 miles from the bridge), it will take you to the mouth of the Owens as it dumps into Crowley Lake. In spring use caution on these roads, the freshly melted snowpack leaves some nasty mudholes and it's not unusual to find a careless angler stranded in one of them. It's a long walk to a phone if you need to call a tow truck out of Mammoth.

In spring you find spawning Kamloops rainbows mixed in with the native rainbows and stocked trout. It's uncommon to find browns in the river at this time, for the most part they stay holed up in Crowley until their fall run.

Early in the season hatches are sparse. Usually in late morning you get an appearance of P.M.D.'s and caddis, this customarily occurs between 11:00 a.m. to about 1:00 p.m.. Of course this all depends on the weather. Later in the season there are good hatches of small blue-winged olives and caddis. At this time you can walk the banks spotting feeding fish, long casts and leaders are required if you want to take these fish on dries. Parachute pattern mayflies and Elk Hair Caddis in sizes 18-20 will deceive the selective feeders.

All season long the river produces good hatches of mayflies, caddis and some stoneflies, but is in fall when the river shines. With the arrival of cooler temperatures comes the fall run rainbows and browns. This is when drifting Woolly Buggers, Matukas and other streamer patterns on 3X tippets along the undercut banks and deep holes produce trophy fish. Starting in August the entire upper part of the Owens comes under special regulations, along with Crowley Lake, to protect spawning trout. You are restricted to flies or artificial lures only, barbless hooks and a two fish of 18 inches or over limit.

Lower Owens River
Long Valley Dam to Bishop

For the purpose of this chapter I call the portion of river from the Long Valley Dam to the five bridges area above the town of Bishop the lower Owens. As the river leaves the dam it flows through a 16 mile section called the Gorge. This portion is reached at the turnoff to Rock Creek that leads to Tom's Place.

Named after Tom Yerby, this resort opened in the 1920s. East of Highway 395 this road runs along the Owens River Gorge. The Gorge is a 700 foot deep gash, cut through the canyon by the Owens River. Most of the river in this area is inaccessible and the lower part before Pleasant Valley Reservoir is interrupted by three hydroelectric plants. You can gain entry to the river in parts of this area but it is risky and dangerous.

This area was known as "Never Fail" in the 1930 to 1940s and is considered one of the greatest fisheries in the West, this changed in the early 1950s. The Department of Water and Power agreed to provide water rights to the Hot Creek hatchery as a trade-off to dewater the Gorge. It was rerouted through silver tubes and headed towards turbines to generate hydroelectricity. This diminished a once great fishery. All remained this way until 1991 when a ruptured pipe in the aqueduct system caused a rewatering of the section. Through litigation, the Department of Water and Power was finally, after 40 years, required to maintain a minimum flow of 16 cfs. This will eventually be increased to 80 cfs. In all likelihood this will happen in a couple of years when the once dry streambed is clear of debris. Hopefully in the future, a once great fishery will return to the status it once held with an earlier generation of fly fishers.

Wild Trout Section

This area of the Owens flows below Pleasant Valley Reservoir, as the river cuts its way along a 200 foot high chalk bluff. The river in this section takes on a different characteristic from the upper section, this portion of the river is a lush, green riparian corridor. Bordered with willows and cottonwoods, the slow water flow screams brown trout to the fly fisher. This section of river is located 6 miles north of Bishop on the Pleasant Valley Road. The wild trout section of the river starts below the footbridge at the campgrounds and continues 4.4 miles downstream to another sign marking its end on Chalk Bluff Road. This section is restricted to zero limit, barbless hook flies or artificial lures only.

Even though this section of river is open to angling all year long, it provides excellent fishing due to the restrictions. This section of the river offers prolific caddis and mayfly hatches during the season. Located nearly 3000 feet lower than Crowley Lake, it provides more consistent hatches in spring due to its milder temperatures. It's not uncommon to find fly fishers traveling to this area out of Mammoth in early season for this very reason.

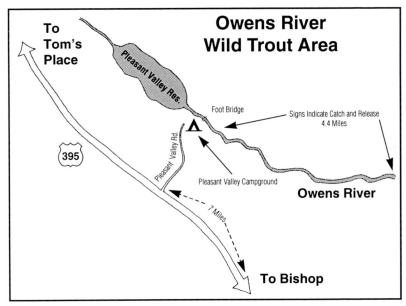

Hot Creek

Rated one of the 10 best dry fly trout streams in America, spending one morning floating dries over the noses of these educated trout and you know why. Hot Creek begins its flow as a warm spring gurgling from the basalt lava table bordering the Hot Creek hatchery. Mammoth Creek runs out of the upper basin lakes and is a tributary to Hot Creek.

From the point of its beginning and along the 15 mile journey to the upper Owens, the river increases both in size and volume. Also along this journey, the waters are subject to a large gathering of anglers trying to entice the resident trout to accept their fur and feather offerings. The upper section below the hatchery is public water flowing unhindered in open meadow land. Cal Trout has plans to add cattle fencing and restore this portion of the creek to bring it to its potential. The river flows through this section and enters the private waters of Hot Creek Ranch (this area is covered in the "Fishing The Ranches" section on page 50).

The lower section returns to public waters below the ranch and cuts its way 2 miles through a deep gorge on its way to the hot springs, for which the creek is named. There are two public parking lots with access to the river below. The water in this section holds open meadows mixed with holding pools and riffles and there is an occasional boulder to provide holding water above and below for trout. Weed growth is heavy in the nutrient-rich water. These weeds hide trout in holding lanes who on opportunity will bolt out to take a drag-free dry fly.

This section of water sees most of the anglers. In the peak of the season it isn't surprising to find both parking lots full. Though the waters are crowded from time to time the anglers for the most part are courteous and respect your fishing area. Unfortunately crowded waters are not uncommon anymore. Hopefully with the rising popularity of fly fishing we will acquire more catch and release quality water to ease pressure on our premium water.

Hot Creek provides the fly angler with a diversity of fishing ranging from excellent nymphing to classic precise dry fly fishing. Most of the season-long hatches are mayflies and caddisflies. Caddis are abundant on this stream, you can walk along the banks during the season and shake thousands of them out of streamside bushes. Hot Creek can also be a gentleman's water. Most of the reliable hatches during the season start around 10:00 a.m. and go until 2:00 p.m. or until the wind kicks up. Evening fishing can also generate nonstop hookups. Be aware that the gates on the road in and out close at sundown.

For you purist dry fly fishermen I am about to make an icono-clastic statement about the classic up and across theory of dry fly fishing. I fish Hot Creek downstream with the dry fly. Not only Hot Creek but all my spring creek fishing I fish downstream. The advantage of this method is that you get a longer drag-free float. Quietly wade upstream above the holding spot and slack cast above the feeding fish and float the fly down to it. Reach across your body at the end of the cast to produce a slack line, this way the fish sees the fly first and not the leader. You can also pull back on the line to adjust the float to get it exactly into the feeding lane. On actively feeding fish you can also pull the fly back above the fish to present it back along the feeding lane to him, of course this is only effective if the dry is still floating. Pull the fly back, away from the target, to drop it back in the feeding lane. I have even reverse tied some of my dry flies to present the fly in a head first position, like the natural, as they float downstream. Not only does this float down like the natural but the thorax and wing hides the hook better. When fishing over selective trout any slight deviance will cause a refusal and when the fish get used to looking at artificials you need to throw them a curve.

Many of the Hot Creek trout are browns. The latest elec-troshock survey conducted by Fish and Game on Hot Creek turned up 11,414 fish per mile. Of these 10,018 were browns and 1,396 were rainbows. In the public section you find nearly all of the fish in the 8 to 16 inch categories. The most popular dry flies are the Elk Hair Caddis, Hemingway Caddis, Olive Parachutes, and Comparaduns. Popular Nymphs are the Pheasant Tail, Hare's Ear, Brassy, Bird's Nest and caddis imitations. In early spring don't over-look tan San Juan Worms, leeches and scud patterns. Another thing that will open the eyes of bankside purists is a Woolly Bugger or rabbit leech stripped downstream across the creek. This can get the attention of fish at the times they ignore other offerings.

San Joaquin River
Middle Fork

Located in Devil's Postpile at an elevation of 7600', the section of the San Joaquin River between Minaret and Rainbow Falls is most favored with fly fishers. This section of river is accessed easily by a gravel highway that has pull outs at Soda Springs, Minaret Falls and the Rainbow Falls trailhead. Skirted by the Pacific Crest Trail the river slips along as a classic trout stream, mixed with runs, riffles and cool dark pools.

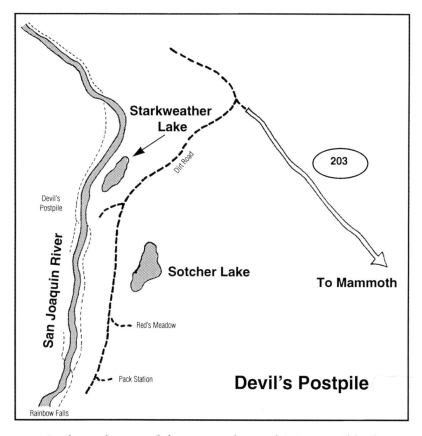

In the early part of the season the road is inaccessible due to winter snows. It usually opens up by June or July, depending on the severity of the previous winter. The opening of the roads to vehicular traffic starts the daily run of the visitors center shuttle bus. When this starts, the Devil's Postpile area is closed to private automobiles and you have to take the shuttle in. That is unless you arrive before 7:30 a.m. and then you can drive your own car in. Usually after Labor Day weekend the summer crowds disappear and along with them the shuttle busses.

During summer months the river has a good flow and wild trout rise readily to dries. These warm months provide excellent dry fly fishing as you jump pool to pool, floating your feathered offering across the slick runs. Royal Wulff's, Humpies and Elk Hair Caddis provoke strikes in every pool they are floated across. This time of season the air is fresh with the scent of pine and you can enjoy the hike as you absorb the visual feast that surrounds you.

As summer passes into fall the water levels drop and the easy days of summer fishing disappear. The lower water concentrates fish into pools and deep undercut banks, a welcome challenge. With the cooler temperatures and the spawning season, the fish become more aggressive. The lower water also makes them more skittish and less likely to rise to a dry. This is when a split-shot weighted nymph, drifted in the undercut banks arouse these trout. In late October the road again becomes subject to closures as an occasional early season snowstorm can dust the area.

Fishing this area is a walk-in affair so travel light. All you need is a pair of hip boots, lightly-packed vest and a fly rod. I hike in a pair of light stocking foot hippers and wading shoes. I have seen some people carrying in their waders but the hike isn't far and walking in hip boots is easygoing. Besides, the less you have to carry the better.

Favorite dry flies for deceiving the wild rainbows and browns are the Adams, Olive Parachute, Elk Hair Caddis, Royal Wulff and Humpies. All in sizes 16-18. Favorite nymphs are Gold Rib Hare's Ear, Pheasant Tail, and Brassies. Also in the 16-18 range.

Still Waters
Lakes of the Mammoth Area
Mammoth Basin Lakes

The basin lakes consist of a string of five lakes that are road accessible and a handfull of others a short walk in. All the lakes are near one another and feed into each other in a chain that eventually drops out of the lower Twin into Mammoth Creek. These lakes are heavily stocked during the peak of the season by the Fish and Game and are also inhabited by a healthy population of wild trout. All the lakes are similar as far as aquatic life and hold rainbows, browns and brookies with a couple even supporting a population of cutthroats. The fly fishing techniques I describe in the following chapters apply to all the basin lakes.

Twin Lakes

This is the first lake you come to as you head up Lake Mary Road out of Mammoth. It is one lake but is actually divided into

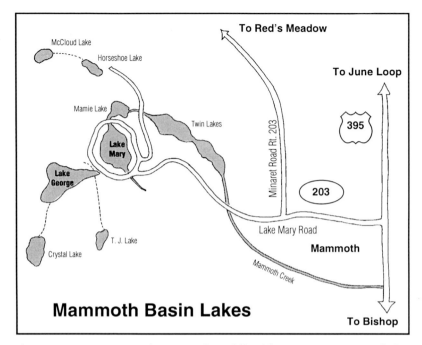

Mammoth Basin Lakes

three sections, upper, lower and middle. The upper section of the lake is fed by the falls flowing out of Mamie Lake. Choked with weeds, travel in a float tube is a bit frustrating at times. While you are cussing these weed beds just remember they are also providing homes for the abundant families of invertebrate, such as damsels, scuds, dragonflies and *Callibaetis.* The interesting thing about these thick weed beds is that they are not native to the lake. Planted in the 1930s by some Bishop sportsmen, they were hoping to enhance the trout fishing conditions by introducing scuds and snails. These plants were collected from Hot Creek and dumped into Twin Lakes. Despite all attempts to get rid of them, fortunately for us and the aquatic life thriving in them, they survive to this day.

Starting with the upper lake area the most productive spot is toward the falls. The water is deeper here due to the falls and the trout are more active in the highly oxygenated, turbulent water that the waterfall produces. To reach this area requires some paddling in a float tube, the only good area to put a tube in is at the boat launch at the opposite end of the lake. It is a small lake and a short five minute paddle will find you in the drop off area.

Because of the abundance of aquatic life in the weed beds, fly fishing is good all season long. Frequent stocking by the Fish and

Game affords some high numbers in the fish catching department during peak season. There are many days when a number 10 Olive Woolly Bugger will produce a strike almost every cast.

The middle portion of the lake sees the least amount of fishing pressure. This is due to the shallower water, four to five feet, and the scarcity of prime trout habitat. During the season fishing in this area is spotty and doesn't generate a lot of attention.

The lower section of the lake on the other hand does split duty with the upper portion, there are days when the upper section is bust and the lower section is wide open. There is only one put-in point for the float tuber and that is the boat launch area at the roadside. This puts you in the shallow area of the lake but a short paddle into the middle puts you into the prime areas. The best fishing is found along the rock slide and the shoreline immediately next to the road.

The Twin is an Odonata lake. The weed beds are thick with damselflies, when the migration starts in late June and through July the trout go into a frenzy. In fact the damselfly is so abundant in this lake you can fish all season with just an Olive Woolly Bugger.

Favored flies for this lake are the Olive Woolly Bugger, Damselfly Nymphs and Matukas. Small mayfly nymphs such as the Gold Ribbed Hare's Ear and the A. P. Nymph in gray or olive or Soft Hackles work in the weed beds. If you want to fish dries the Adams, Sierra Bright Dot and Griffith's Gnats in the smaller sizes seduce trout in shallow areas.

Lake Mary

Heading up Lake Mary Road past Twin Lakes you come to the Lake Mary turn off. This is the largest of the Mammoth lakes, about a mile long. Local legend has it that Mary and Mamie Lakes were named after Bodie dance-hall girls. The road loops around the lake and comes back out on the highway. The best spot to float tube the lake is the stump area right off the Lake Mary turn off, on the eastern shore of the lake. There is a ledge drop off about a 100 yards off the shoreline that is good.

Mary is the most popular of the lakes and is an excellent fly fishing lake. The resident population of trout is heavily supplemented during the season with hatchery fish and Alper's rainbows in the two- to six-pound range. It is not uncommon to be stripping a Woolly Bugger and have your quiet morning interrupted by a three pound, airborne rainbow.

Since this lake does not have the thick weeds that the Twin

Lakes have the damselflies are not as thick. They are still the dominant aquatic lifeform in the lake, as evidenced by the effectiveness of the Olive Woolly Bugger and Damselfly pattern. The Matuka is also a popular pattern. As far as fishing dries the Mosquito and Adams in 16-18 are popular, these flies work better in the shallower shoreline areas and around the stumps.

Lake George, Mamie and Horseshoe

I clumped these lakes together because they are not as productive to the fly fisher and therefore not as popular. Below Mary is Mamie, the other lake believed to be named after a Bodie dance-hall girl. It is a shallow lake and the inlet area where Lake Mary flows into Mamie being the most popular spot. This area produces the best from midsummer on and during late October it is not uncommon to find a few good browns in this area.

Lake George is just above Mary at 9,006 feet and is the highest of the road accessible lakes in the Mammoth group. The lake is also up to 200 feet deep which makes fly fishing only effective in the shallower shoreline areas.

Horseshoe Lake is the last one in the group where the road ends 10 miles from US 395. Because this lake sits over porous, volcanic rock the water level varies considerably throughout the year. During the season the declining water level makes it necessary to get to the deeper water in the center of the lake. As desolate as this lake looks, it does hold a good population of brook trout.

Backcountry Lakes

Located a half-mile walk on the Horseshoe Lake trailhead is McCloud Lake. This easily accessible lake does not see a lot of pressure. It is a Lahontan cutthroat lake now and then stocked by the Fish and Game. It sports a no-kill, barbless-only regulation that helps keep it a quality fishery.

Favorite flies are small mayfly nymphs, Woolly Buggers and damselfly patterns. Dries are the Sierra Bright Dot, Royal Wulff, Mosquito and Griffith's Gnat in small sizes.

Above Lake George to the southwest are Crystal and T. J. Lakes. Both lakes are a short hike in and are abundant with brook trout in the 8 to 10 inch ranges.

At the Coldwater campground south of Mary Lake you will find the trail that leads to six lakes: Heart, Arrowhead, Woods, Skeleton, Red and Barney. All of the lakes afford good fishing for small brookies and rainbows and can be fished in a day-hike.

Crowley Lake

Home of the tackle busters, goes the saying with the old-timers. This lake is the gem of the Eastern Sierra. As you drive past on Highway 395, it doesn't appear inviting. A barren, treeless shoreline with alkali dust devil's sporadically swirling across the surrounding sagebrush prairie. It is also said you can walk across the lake stepping from boat-to-boat on opening weekend. With many families, it is a long-standing tradition to make the opener on Crowley Lake. The first time you fish this lake, it will get into your bloodstream. This body of water produces big trout consistently, from 1971 to 1983 the state record brown trout of twenty-five pounds, eleven ounces was held by this lake. Once thought to be a trophy fishery only during the fall season, fly fishers are finding good fishing all season.

In 1941 the Department of Water and Power completed the Long Valley Dam across the Owens River and filled the lowest portion of Long Valley creating Crowley Lake. In doing so they flooded a meadow area that had been used as pasture for Owens Valley cattle. The lake gathers water from the upper Owens River and sends it down to an arid Los Angeles. The lake is named after father J. J. Crowley, who struggled to get the Owens Valley residents to overcome their bitterness after the "water wars" with Los Angeles. He was the area's biggest promoter before his death in a tragic auto accident in 1940.

Rainbows and browns inhabit the lake. Over the years the Fish and Game have introduced many species of rainbows and the lake is now dominated by three specific strains. Fish and Game has clipped different fins on the introduced rainbows to make identification easy. This allows them to study the various strains to see which survive best in the lake's ecosystem.

If the fish has a left ventral fin clipped it is a Kamloops introduced from the Junction Reservoir. If the right ventral fin is clipped it is a Coleman rainbow that is a steelhead strain from the Shasta hatchery. If the adapose fin is clipped it is an Eagle Lake rainbow. If none of the fins are clipped it is likely that your fish is a wild one spawned in some tributary of the Owens River. Most rainbows average one to two pounds. There is also a good mix of three pounders and an occasional five pounder thrown in.

Although not caught in the same numbers as rainbows there is a good population of browns that don't really make a good showing until the fall season. Browns in the lake seem to average around two pounds, with a good mix of six to eight pounders. One fall a few years ago, the Fish and Game electroshocked a 20-pound brown in

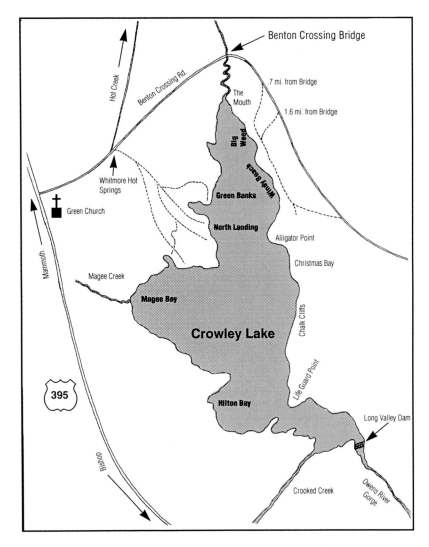

Benton Crossing Bridge

Hot Creek

Benton Crossing Rd.

.7 mi. from Bridge

The Mouth

1.6 mi. from Bridge

Big Weed

Whitmore Hot Springs

Windy Beach

Green Banks

Green Church

North Landing

Alligator Point

Mammoth

Christmas Bay

Magee Creek

Magee Bay

Crowley Lake

Chalk Cliffs

395

Life Guard Point

Hilton Bay

Long Valley Dam

Bishop

Crooked Creek

Owens River Gorge

the mouth of the Owens River. There are plenty of "Big Moe" stories, anyone who has fished the lake regularly has at least one Moe story. It's the strike that has your rod tip slapping the water, a reel screeching run and then the fish is gone before you know what happened. More than once I have seen an angler sitting in their float tube, head hanging down, pounding the sides of the tube with their fists in disbelief of the event that has just occurred.

The trout growth rate in the lake is remarkable. A trout introduced at the beginning of the season will gain a pound to a pound and a half by the close of the season. The reason for this is the many Sacramento perch that inhabit the lake, when the perch minnows start to show in the weed beds in late summer the trout go into a feeding frenzy. They were illegally introduced into the lake in the early sixties by some live bait fishermen, since then they have established residence in the lake and even provide sport to a growing number of High Sierra perch anglers. The state record Sacramento perch of three pounds, ten ounces comes from Crowley. It is this fish that creates the exciting trout fishing that the lake has to offer. There is nothing more heart stopping than having a big trout race out of a weed bed chasing your Matuka, mistaking it for an easy meal.

Another factor of the prosperity of the lake is the abundance of midges. This chironomid hatches year-round and provides an endless feast for the trout, they love to cruise the surface feeding on them. Fishing for them when they are in this feeding pattern can drive even the most patient fly fisherman mad. They roll on the surface of the slack water near the shoreline, sipping in emergers with no consistent pattern. They become selective and you have to cast your rear off to get one to take. It is tough fishing but not without its rewards.

Damselflies are also important players in the food chain. When the weed beds become abundant in July, they become homes to these wiggly trout morsels. Although they don't appear as significant as on the concentrated waters of the basin lakes it is still a food source that the trout key on. It is the variety of feed in this fertile eight-mile lake that presents the angler with many opportunities.

Other aquatic insects of lesser importance are the caddis and mayflies. Only the *Callibaetis* hatch's with consistency in the waters of Crowley. The smaller mayflies and caddis need moving water and hatch in the waters of the upper Owens and float down into the lake. They are found in the headwaters around Green Banks at the mouth of the Owens.

The best way for the fly fisher to fish the lake is from a float tube. You limit yourself by fishing from the shore. Boats are allowed on the lake and there is also a rental marina but fishing from a float tube is by far the most popular. It is so popular, there are weekends in fall where the waters at Green Banks look like a bowl of Cheerios. The float tube allows more stealth and maneuverability in the weeds. A large percentage of your fishing will be subsurface, with wet flies, nymphs or streamers. Your fishing techniques will vary, depending on the time of the year. It can be with a sink-tip in weed beds or trolling along with a full sinker when there is no activity on the surface. The only time you will find a dry line useful is when fishing the "gulpers." The trick to fishing a pod feeding on the midge hatch is to pick one fish and target it. Decide the direction he is moving and lead him with your cast. If you have done it right the fish will "gulp" your fly as he moves along sipping midges off the surface.

During the season the lake goes through distinct changes. In spring most trout are found closer to the shore, spring spawning Kamloops cruise the shoreline in great numbers. For the most part you are trolling around in the float tube trying to locate the roving pods. Later in the season around August through September the weed beds get thick and the fish are easier to locate. They like to cruise around in the weeds becoming opportunistic feeders on the perch fry and invertebrate life that the weed beds support. Fishing at this time is sight fishing and for the fly fisherman this is the most exciting type of fishing there is. It is also time to go to the heavier 2X leaders. The trout are in an aggressive attack mode and strikes are powerful.

Come October the lake again changes its character. The weed beds are disappearing, scattering the trout habitat. In the fall this lake requires a different mode of operation. Gone are the 6X tippets, floating lines and soft hackle patterns, now it's time to get serious. Put on the heavy tippets, sinking line, streamer flies and hold on. When was the last time you've seen a heavyweight fighter getting ready for a title match by eating rice cakes? The same holds true for the trout in Crowley. The big fish don't want any small midge fly, they want meat! And they don't mess around. In fall they are in training for the oncoming winter and bulking up to survive it. These are the days of the aggressive trout strikes, the strikes that try to rip the rod from your hand and have the tip slapping the water. You know, the kind that give you temporary cardiac arrest. Don't be surprised to get one of these strikes, a quick run and the fly spit back in your face. This is the character of the hogs. When hooked they know the tricks, such as running toward you faster than you can strip the line in. Or jumping like a tuna and porpoising around your tube. If you do all the right things you are sometimes rewarded with an eighteen plus inch trout. Twenty to twenty four inch trout are not uncommon in the fall season.

Crowley has several miles of accessible shoreline but the most productive and favorite area for the float-tuber is the north end where the upper Owens dumps into the lake. The western side is the Green Banks and North Landing area. You reach this area by taking Benton Crossing Road (Green Church on the corner) of Highway 395. Take the second dirt road turn off to the right past Whitmore Hot Springs. After 1.25 miles on the dirt road, you will come to a cattle gate. Go through (making sure to close the gate behind you) and keep to the left to end at Green Banks. Go straight to reach North Landing Bay.

To reach the eastern side of the lake, keep going straight on Benton Crossing Road, crossing the bridge over the Owens River. Take the third dirt road turn off 1.6 miles from the bridge. This road takes you along the Owens River, on to the mouth and access to the Windy Beach and Leighton Springs area.

Sotcher Lake

Sotcher is located in the Red's Meadow, Devil's Postpile area. It's a great place to combine with a trip to the San Joaquin River. It also makes a good, quiet get-away lake when you want a break from the weekend crowds at the other lakes. The lake sits in an area carved out of granite eons ago by glacier activity. Fishable shoreline is limited and a float tube is required to effectively fly fish the lake.

Sotcher holds a good population of rainbow, brook and brown trout. Since it is not catch and release, or a restricted method of take body of water, it gets supplemented with trout by Fish and Game during the season. One spring a few years ago, I saw a ten pound brown come out of this lake.

Being a small lake there isn't one area that produces better than another. The lake is fed by Sotcher Creek as it enters the lake through a beaver dam. If you fish the lake in the morning you find active pods of fish feeding on the surface. A small wet fly, such as a Woolly Bugger or small nymphs, cast into these pods produces trout. Once the sun crests the mountain and its rays hit the lake the surface feeding trout disappear. You now have two choices: Troll the lake with wet flies and small streamers or go fish the San Joaquin River. I usually pick the latter. It makes for a great morning in the Devil's Postpile area and you can always stop to fish the lake again on your way out.

Sotcher is reached by taking Highway 203 out of Mammoth to Devil's Postpile. It is reached by the road to Red's Meadow and located on the left side of the road. There is a small parking lot with public restrooms and a picnic area. Below the parking lot is a small beach area that allows easy access by float tube into the lake.

Heenan Lake

Although it is not located in the Mammoth area, but in Alpine County, I feel it should be included in the book. This is a favorite area with local fly fishers and when the limited season opens they fish it frequently. It is a zero-kill, cutthroat brood-stock lake owned by the Department of Fish and Game. Some of the eggs from these brooders are supplied to the Hot Creek hatchery. It was opened to the public in 1984 to see what effect catch and release fishing would have on the fish. You can only use barbless flies or lures only. There is also a three-dollar entrance fee to fish here and it is open only Friday through Sunday starting on the Friday before Labor day and continuing through the last Sunday in October.

You can fish the hundred-acre lake from the shoreline, boat (electric motors only) or float tube. It is a great place to experience the tug of a 26 inch cutthroat. Fish in the 20 to 30 inch range are not uncommon.

The best flies are big Woolly Buggers, the saying is any color works as long as its black. A proficient fly fisher can release unreal numbers of trout in one day. Although these are not the picky trout you find in a spring creek you still have to work for them.

To reach Heenan Lake you take Highway 395 north past Bridgeport and turn left on State 89 near Markleeville. The lake is reached by going south on a small, unmarked dirt road, four miles from the junction of Highway 89 and 4. It is about an hour and a half to two hour drive from Mammoth but well worth the trip.

Thoughts on Tubing

Of all the ways to fish in this quiet sport called fly fishing, float tubing is my favorite. Unlike stream, river or flats fishing where you are an observer of your environment, in tubing you become a part of it. It's feeling the water temperature and current and becoming a part of the aquatic insect cycle when a *Callibaetis* or damselfly crawls onto your tube to dry its newly hatched wings.

Frenzied trout chase a meal and dodge your flippers. Ducklings follow the tube thinking you are family. Fall flights of waterfowl fly noisily over making their way south. It's the early morning sounds of the teal's wingtips as they slice through the morning air. Becoming a part of the early morning mist as you slip into the water. It's joining the weed bed environment, probing the channels in pursuit of trout. At times being the center of a feeding pod jumping and splashing around you.

Unlike a stream where trout habitat exposes itself in runs, riffles and pools, lakes hold their secrets making you work hard to reveal them.

Lake dwelling trout are fat, fast and feisty. They can rip a good run off your reel without the help of a downstream current. They can hit the fly so hard your rod tip slaps the water.

They jump two feet from your tube and spit the fly in your face. When released they ungratefully flip their tail at you splashing water in the rush to freedom.

You experience the cold morning and after dark paddles back to the shore with only a flashlight to lead the way. The hooked fat trout dancing around your float tube and silence so still the ears ring. The unexplainable feelings of releasing a huge rainbow where you have to sit a minute to absorb the passing event, then you will understand.

This is my world of float tubing. I love all aspects of fly fishing but these are the things that bring me back to the tube.

Pay-to-Play
The Private Ranches
Alper's Owens River Ranch

Alper's is the first of the two pay-to-play ranches located on the upper Owens River. The ranch is located 15 miles north of Mammoth Lakes and four miles down Owens River Road. It is a 300-acre cattle ranch deeded to the Alper's family in 1869. The main lodge was built in the late 1800s or early 1900s, no one knows for sure. To walk into the main lodge is to walk into the past. The ceilings are low and you want to duck your head as you enter, to say the place is unique would be an understatement. It is downright earthy and uncomplicated, they get their water from a well and produce their own electricity. In the past it was known as a rustic hide-a-way for some Hollywood types. Actors such as Jane Russell, Hugh O'Brian and Robert Blake were regular visitors here. Not only do trout spawn here but T.V. shows we watched in our past were also spawned here. The writers for "Father Knows Best" and "My Three Sons" used to hole up on the ranch and do a seasons worth of writing.

Two miles of the Owens River snakes through the meadows of the ranch, this section of river is wild trout water, with resident rainbows and browns and migratory trout traveling upstream from Crowley to spawn. The ranch water is designated fly fishing only.

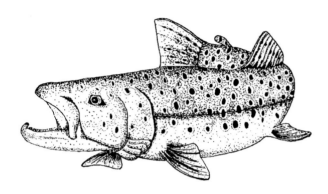

There is also two miles of man-made stream known as Alper's Creek. The creek is stocked with fish from the ranch's hatchery and has a two fish limit if you are so inclined.

The ranch also has its own hatchery operation. Tim Alper's raises Coleman rainbows, a steelhead strain from Lassen County. He feeds them 70,000 pounds of high-grade trout chow a year and harvests 90,000 eggs a year. He takes these eggs and in three years he nurtures them into five to ten pound fish, these fish are then introduced into the Mammoth area waters. Alper's rainbows are well-known among the Mammoth area anglers. The goal of Tim Alper is to make Mono County known as the spot in California for trophy trout. He is also cross-breeding different species in an attempt to produce a large, hard fighting trout.

New to the ranch is a three-and-a-half acre pond that has spent two years in the planning stage. The pond is stocked with trout that run over the ten pound mark. The pond is similar to the private ponds found in Washington and Oregon but on a smaller scale. Fishing is for ranch guests only. It is also limited to float tube fly fishing only, with no more than two anglers on the pond at one time and it is strictly catch and release.

The ranch water supports a good hatch of mayflies but caddis are the bread and butter hatch. This hatch is a dependable season-long happening. The nature of the river is slow and meandering with undercuts. The early part of the season is mostly nymph fishing and throwing streamers to the spring run rainbows. During summer months, remarkable caddis hatches provide the dry fly fishing this area is well-known for.

Accommodations at the ranch are all housekeeping cabins. All amenities are included, all you bring is gear and food. Beer, pop and some limited groceries are available at the ranch lodge. There are nine cabins and their sizes vary, they can sleep two to ten people. The rates start at 35 dollars a day. The most popular time is the fall season and is usually booked a year in advance. Reservations can be made by writing Alper's Owens River Ranch, Rt.1, Box 232, Mammoth Lakes, CA. 93546 or call, summer (619) 934-2232 or winter (619) 647-6652.

Arcularius Ranch

Bordering Alper's, Arcularius is the next ranch you come to on Owens River Ranch Road. This ranch is the counterpart of Alper's. Whereas Alper's is funky, Arcularius is a neatly manicured and painted operation. It is a perfect spot for the fly fisher who wants to bring along a nonfishing spouse for a get-away. It is an 1,080-acre ranch that runs around 100 head of cattle. More importantly for the fly fisher five miles of the upper Owens winds through the property. The ranch is run under a catch and release, fly fishing only policy.

The ranch's water is a perfect representation of classic spring creek water. Winding through treeless brushy meadow, the slow-moving water provides habitat for a myriad of caddis, mayflies and small stoneflies. This whole stretch of the upper Owens also sports a good population of scuds.

The ranch affords enough water that even when fully booked, it is not uncommon to have a stretch of water all to yourself. As with the other ranches there have been generations of anglers that have stayed here. Browsing about in the main cabin built in 1938, the faded photographs reveal old-time anglers sporting smiles and stringers of huge trout.

Like with all the water of the upper Owens, fly selection is the same. Recommended dries are Elk Hair Caddis sizes 14-20, Hemmingway Caddis sizes 14-20, Olive Parachute sizes 16-20. Favorite nymphs are the Hare's Ear sizes 12-18. Pheasant Tail sizes 12-18, A. P. series nymphs in gray or tan sizes 14-18, Soft Hackles sizes 12-16 and the chamois caddis nymph is deadly on this stretch of water in sizes 12-18. Other "must have" patterns are scuds sizes 12-14 and Zug Bugs in 10-14. In summer make sure you have a good hopper and ant pattern in your fly box.

Big trout are prevalent in the water on the ranch, four to eight pound browns and rainbow are recorded season long. The area is not stocked and all fish are of natural spawn. Water on "The Arc" is well managed as to the number of rods allowed on the water and wading the stream other than to cross the river is not allowed.

All cabins on the ranch are housekeeping units and equipped with stove, refrigerator, cooking utensils and linens. Some cabins have enclosed porches that make warm summer evenings enjoyable and bug-free. Groceries, beer and soft drinks are available in the main lodge. A two-day minimum stay is required and the rates start at sixty dollars per night.

For more information they can be reached by writing Arcularius Ranch, Rt. 1, Box 230, Mammoth Lakes, CA. 93546 or call (619) 648-7807 (summer), (805) 239-3830 (winter).

Hot Creek

Hot Creek is the purist's nirvana. The rules here are very simple—catch and release, barbless hooks, dry flies only. No nymph fishing is allowed. No sir, this is dry fly water. It is the only section of water in the United States so designated. You can feel the spirit of Halford as you float delicate, drag-free dry flies in the gin clear water of Hot Creek. The dry fly only rule has been in effect since 1950 at the suggestion of a Fish and Game biologist. Even with these tough rules anglers come from as far away as Japan, New Zealand, Britain and France to fish here.

The water of Hot Creek is fertile and provides a 365 day hatch. The reason for this is the constant year-round water temperature of 56 to 60 degrees. The headwaters of Hot Creek is a surge of thermal water that springs up through a basalt lava table. The ranch property starts just a mile downstream from this source.

The Hot Creek area was used by native Paiute Indians before the area was homesteaded as a cattle ranch in the late 1800s. An avid fly fisherman named Roy Bateman bought the 248-acre spread in 1937 and his descendants opened the ranch to guests in 1955. The cattle were removed in 1973 because of the negative effect they had on the stream, at the same time they also banned any wading.

This is technical water that requires stealth and concentration on the anglers part. The ranch owns 2.5 miles of the creek that sports slick glassy runs, carpeted with dense braids of aquatic weeds. It is also peppered with a cobblestone and gravel bottom that provides excellent spawning redds for resident trout. The weeds are home for the abundant aquatic insect life that inhabits the river. Caddis and mayflies are the most dominant hatches. The most popular flies are the Hemingway Caddis sizes 16-20, Elk Hair Caddis sizes 16-20, Light Cahill sizes 16-20, Parachute Adams sizes 16-20, Pale Evening Dun sizes 18-20, Red Quill sizes 16-20. August through October the Trico hatch goes off and the CDC Trico Dun and spinner in sizes 18-22 do the job.

Although brown and rainbow are the trout that dwell in these waters, it is the hard-to-please brown that makes up 70 percent of the population. The official ranch record is a fourteen pound, eleven ounce brown trout. Trout more than 20 inches are not uncommon and 13 to 15 inchers are standard. For the most part sight fishing for rising trout is the norm. The fish see many flies drifted over their heads and the clear water requires the use of long leaders. Twelve to sixteen feet, with a 6X or 7X tippet is standard.

Hot Creek Ranch is located just east of Highway 395 on Hot Creek Hatchery Road five miles south of Mammoth Lakes. They have nine housekeeping cottages located a stone's throw from the creek. They allow no more than three anglers per cabin and that means no more than 27 anglers can be working the stream at one time. They all have enclosed porches, carports and beautiful views. Each cabin has two double beds, bedding, linen, dishes and utensils. Rates are 87 dollars per day, $515 per week double occupancy. For more information contact: Hot Creek Ranch, Rt. 1, Box 206, Mammoth Lakes, CA. 93546, (619) 935-4214.

Guides

Over the past years, I have always used a guide to fish waters I am not familiar with. When you fish an area new to you, hiring a guide to help you along is a good idea. I found all of the guides I have used to be professional and knowledgeable about the area they are guiding. After all this is why you hire a guide. They should also be courteous and friendly. There are exceptions to the rule, such as in the Florida Keys. These guys yell at clients as a rule, there seems to be something about triple digit tarpon that gets them excited. Guides are up on the latest tackle, and are experienced fly tiers and usually hold a couple of secret patterns in their vest.

A good way to pick a guide is to talk to somebody who has fished the area with one. Or visit a well-known fly shop in the area, good shops have good guides. Their livelihood depends on it. Another plus to using guides from a shop is that they all share infor-

mation and that gives you, the client, the best opportunities for your day of fishing.

What to Expect

Your guide should give you information before your trip. He can tell you what tackle is needed for the water you are fishing; and unless you have booked months in advance, what type of water conditions and hatches to expect. At this time it is also important for you to let the guide know your preferences. Do you prefer dry fly fishing as opposed to nymphs? This will influence the type of water and the areas the guide will take you on. Be up-front with the guide as far as any physical conditions that might limit the area you can fish. Maybe you have a bum ankle and cannot wade deep in fast water. It is important to remember to fish through the guide, always listen and don't let your ego get in the way. Relax, observe and listen. Don't try to second guess the guide. If you do this he will feel you don't really need his help and you are wasting everyone's time.

The morning you meet he will probably suggest a few patterns that are working on the particular stretch of water you will be fishing. Trust him, selling a few flies is not a life or death matter to him but it will help with your success on the water. Remember, you have already spent hundreds of dollars to get there and hire a guide, not counting the money you have invested on tackle. Your guide enjoys a successful day, just as much as you do.

What is Expected of You

Have a positive attitude! Don't be afraid to ask many questions. A guided trip not only affords you a fishing opportunity but also a chance to savor some local nature and history. You should also have a very good handle on your casting. Once you are on the water, it is no time to practice. For example, if you know beforehand you are going to be floating a river in a drift boat and quick accurate casts are required, then practice weeks before your trip. You should be able to land a fly in a ten inch circle at fifty feet.

Don't treat the guide as your personal servant, he is a professional and should be treated accordingly. Your guide has dedicated much time and sweat into making this a livelihood, it is done out of love of the water, fish and the sport. Don't expect him to tie a new fly on for you every time you lose one. This is not a fishing contest between you and the guide, I have even known guides who do not carry a rod. The guide should be concentrating his efforts and time on the client. But if the fishing is going great, don't be afraid to ask him to pick up a rod and join in.

If the guide has shown you a good day and you are satisfied with his efforts be sure to tip. The average tip is between 10 and 15 percent but if you feel he is worth more and you can afford it, don't hesitate.

When time is precious to you, especially your time on the water, you should consider using a guide at least once. It is the best way for a person with limited time, or a newcomer to the sport, to maximize his fishing time.

Part Three: Hatches and the Seasons

Mammoth Area Hatches

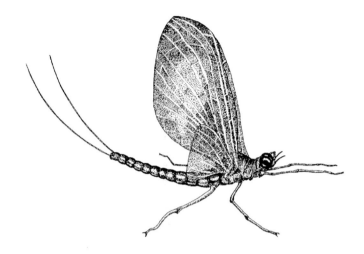

Mayflies
Ephemeroptera

No other aquatic insect has been discussed and written about as much as the mayfly. The sight of this delicate insect floating along with glassy upright wings is a vision etched in the memory of many anglers. There are three stages to a mayflies' life: nymph, dun and spinner.

The nymph has three tails of equal length and gills on the abdomen. They are usually a pale green, mottled olive or shades of gray depending on the general coloration of their surroundings.

The dun is the first stage of the adult mayfly. It is sexually immature and has two or three tails, the wings are opaque and sometimes marked.

The spinner is the final stage of the adult mayfly after the dun has shed its outer skin. The glossy spinners have clear wings, large eyes and long forelegs. This is the sexually mature adult that mates and returns to the water to deposit its eggs. The males die a few days after mating. The females expire after egglaying and can be seen on the water with outstretched wings.

Mammoth Area Hatches

Hatch	May	June	July	Aug.	Sept.	Oct.	Patterns
Mayfly							
Baetis	■	■					P.T. Nymph/B.W.O. Para
Ephemereaella			■				Hare's Ear/Pale Morn. Dun
Paraleptophlebia	■						P.T. Nymph/Red Quill
Callibaetis			■	■			Hare's Ear/Adams
Baetis divinctus				■			P.T. Nymph/Red Quill
Tricorythodes				■	■		Trico Spin./Trico Para
Baetis vagens						■	Zug Bug/Adams
Stonefly							
Isoperla			■				B. Nest/Ltl Yellow Stone
Caddis							
Limnephilidae		■					Peeking Caddis/Elk Hair
Hydropsyche		■	■				Olive Hares Ear/Elk Hair
Glossomoma			■	■			Bird's Nest/Elk Hair
Rhyacophila			■				Cham. Nymph/Elk Hair
Brachycentrus					■		P.T. Nymph/Elk Hair
Midge							
Chironomid	■	■	■	■	■	■	M. Pupa/Mosquito/Adams
Damselfly							
Zygoptera		■	■				Mar. Damsel/W. Bugger
Terrestrials							
Hoppers				■	■		Dave's Hopper
Crickets					■		Dave's Cricket
Beetles					■		Blk. Deer Hair Beetle
Ants			■				McMurry Ant

Emergence (Approx.)

Baetis: Blue-Winged Olive

This hatch welcomes the fly fisher into the season and turns over the closed sign at the end of the season. This is a swimmer and one of the most common mayflies found in running water. They are abundant in swift, clean, freestone streams. Biologists have found that the *Baetis* is capable of multiple broods during a season, this means they can hatch sporadically at any part of the season.

Patterns: Nymphs sizes 12-18, Gold Ribbed Hare's Ear, Pheasant Tail. Dry fly, sizes 12-18 B.W.O. Parachute, Olive No Hackle.

Ephemerella: Pale Morning Dun

This mayfly is one of the most important hatches of the West. It is found in slow-moving spring creeks and quicker moving rivers. The *E. inermis* olive yellow duns hatch in the Mammoth area from mid-June through July. Depending on the previous year's winter weather conditions, it is an abundant hatch in the Sierra. It is one of the most documented hatches in angling literature making it popular with the western angler.

Patterns: Nymph sizes 14-18, Gold Ribbed Hare's Ear, Pheasant Tail. Dry flies, sizes 14-18 Pale Morning Dun, Adams.

Paraleptophlebia: Mahogany Dun

Not one of the more important hatches in the Mammoth area it only occurs on smaller creeks. It does hatch on Hot Creek, so it is important to have a few imitations in your fly box. This hatch occurs early in May on Hot Creek due to its warmer water. Other waters of the Sierra find a later emergence time usually around late May and into June. This hatch overlaps with the Blue-Winged Olives. It is an early morning hatch and produces a spectacular late evening spinner fall. This is also a favorite hatch of the dry fly fisher. The duns float a long distance during the emergence making them easy targets for trout.

Patterns: Nymphs sizes 12-16, Gold Ribbed Hare's Ear, Pheasant Tail, Bird's Nest. Dry flies, 12-16 Red Quill.

Callibaetis: Speckled Dun

Most abundant in lakes or ponds, principally in those abundant with vegetation, the nymphs are three tailed and larger than the *Baetis.* In the Mammoth area there are usually two to three hatches during the season, the hatches start around July and continue into September. The adult dries are distinguished by gray wings with dark markings and small hind wings.

Patterns: Nymphs sizes 12-16, Hare's Ear or Pheasant Tail. Dry flies, sizes 12-18 Adams or Gray Quill.

Tricorythodes: Trico

This is the late season fly. It is also the fly that will test your eyesight because you have to use a size 18-22 to imitate the natural. Even in the best of light this minute-sized fly is trying to the angler when knotting it on his 7X tippet. When you do finally get it tied on you then have to be able to see it on the water to know when the fish takes. This hatch occurs around August through September in the Mammoth area.

Patterns: Nymphs, none. Dry flies, sizes 20-24 Black and White Trico Spinner, Olive Trico Spinner.

Stonefly
Plecoptera
Isoperla: Little Yellow Stone

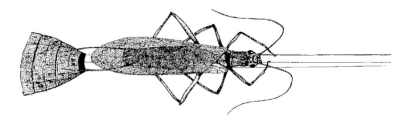

The stonefly is not one of the most abundant hatches in the Mammoth area. Some waters in the area such as Hot Creek do not even have a hatch to speak of. Unlike the larger species of stonefly such as the *Pteronarcys, Isoperla* is a smaller species. The adults are a size 10 at the largest.

They are most commonly found in the Owens River, with the lower section supporting the largest population. Stonefly hatches are legendary in other places in the country but unfortunately they are not major hatches in the Mammoth area. The emergence period is usually from mid-June through July.

Patterns: Nymph, sizes 10-18 Bird's Nest, Adult, sizes 10-18 Little Yellow Stone or yellow Elk Hair Caddis.

Caddisflies
Trichoptera

Next to the Chironomid this is the most abundant hatch in the Mammoth Lakes area. You can walk the banks of Hot Creek and kick thousands of caddis from the streamside bushes. It is also common to see a multitude of cases from *Limnephilidae* sticking to the sides of your float tube where the water of the Owens flows into Crowley. Most all species of caddis build cases out of gravel and stream vegetation. Similar to the midge, the caddis goes through a four-stage metamorphosis: Egg, larva, pupa, adult. The larva has several molts during its stage and has to build new cases to fit the larger size. After the final molt the larva then seals itself into its case and transforms into the pupa stage. When it's time to emerge the pupa will free itself from the case and rise rapidly to the surface via the gas trapped in its exoskelton. Trout feeding on these rapidly emerging caddis can be spotted by their splashy, noisy rise. The newly emerged adults skitter across the surface of the water in their attempt to reach the freedom of streamside vegetation.

Adult caddis are identified by their tent-like wing that lays back over the body. Adults are most advantageous to fly fishers when females return to the water to deposit their eggs. They bounce along the water's surface trying to break the tension to lay their eggs, this bobbing dance over the water's surface drives trout wild.

Limnephilidae: Sedge

This is the larger species of the caddis family. Commonly found in the Owens River and Hot Creek, the larva builds a tube-shaped case of twigs, gravel and pine needles. Emergence usually occurs in June and into July. This period usually starts a few weeks earlier on Hot Creek due to its warm, thermally-heated water.

Pattern: Subsurface, 8-10 Peeking Caddis. Adult, 10-12 Elk Hair Caddis.

Hydropsyche: Spotted Sedge

The larva of this species does not build a case, instead it hooks itself to the stream bottom by a thin silk thread. It is found in all moving water of the Mammoth area, common to slow meadow rivers as well as quick flowing freestone mountain streams. The larva is identified by the brushy gills on the underside of its abdomen. Body colors range from green to tan.

The adult has a brown body covered with a mottled brown wing. After mating, females oviposit their eggs by swimming to the bottom and gluing them to rocks.

Pattern: Subsurface, 10-14 Olive Hare's Ear or Rockworm, Adult, 10-16 Elk Hair Caddis.

Glossosoma: Saddle-Case Maker

The larva of this species builds its case out of pebbles on the stream bottom, they attach themselves to the stones just under the waterline. The larva requires cold, well-oxygenated water found in the Mammoth area.

The hatch period for *Glossosoma* starts late May and continues sporadically into early August. During the egg laying cycle the female adult penetrates the water's surface to attach her eggs to the stream bottom and then thrashes in the current until it drowns or becomes easy prey for trout.

This is not a large species of the caddis family but its abundance and long hatch cycle make it an important food in the Mammoth area.

Pattern: Subsurface, size 16-18 Bird's Nest, Adult, size 16-18 Elks Hair.

Rhyacophila: Olive Sedge

This caddis does not build a case, instead it traverses along the stream bottom on a strand of silk, foraging freely on smaller aquatic foods. This characteristic makes them easy targets for foraging trout.

The larva is of green, brown or gray coloration and its emergence period usually starts around mid-June and continues through July.

Patterns: Subsurface, size 10-18 Chamois Nymph or Green Rockworm. Adult, size 10-18 Elk Hair Caddis.

Brachycentrus: Grannom

The larva of this species build square, tapered cases out of aquatic plant material. You can find clustered colonies of these larva in stream bottom rocks where they are huddled feeding on small aquatic organisms and plant matter that flow past them. Pupation usually occurs in slower, weedy shallows where they attach themselves to sticks or deadfalls before emergence.

Female adults return to highly-oxygenated areas of the stream, such as riffles, to oviposit. They can be seen in the evening dipping over the water depositing their egg clusters. The hatch usually occurs in the Mammoth area starting in late August and getting more consistent in September then tapering off by early October.

Patterns: Subsurface, 10-18 Pheasant Tail or Peeking Caddis, Adult, 12-18 Elk Hair.

Midge
Chironomid

The midge is most abundant in lakes, ponds or streams with a heavy growth of aquatic plants. Like the caddis, the midge goes through a complete metamorphosis: Egg, larva, pupa and adult. The larvae resembles a small, thin red worm. An adult midge looks similar to a mosquito (same family), except they don't bite. It is a season-long hatch in the Sierra and the adult midge can be seen in huge swarms along the banks of Crowley Lake. Some anglers mistake them for mosquitoes as they hover in the warm air radiating from the surface of their parked vehicles. God bless the midge. They are in great abundance and the trout love them.

When the pupa breaks the surface tension of the water to hatch you see the bulging rise of trout as they feed. Pods of trout cruise the surface sipping in the hatching insects. This can drive an angler batty because they break the surface in no predictable pattern and become very selective. Repeated casts will produce nothing but successive refusals. It is impossible to ignore active feeding trout, so you just keep torturing yourself cast after cast. Keep at it, every once in a while a fish will pounce on your offering.

Occasionally trout work the shoreline weed beds feeding on adult midges. This is a common occurance in the basin lakes and a small size 14-16 Adams or mosquito dryfly entice these shoreline cruisers into striking.

Damselflies
Zygoptera

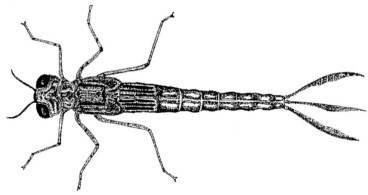

Damselfly nymphs can be found in great abundance in the basin lakes and are also quite common in Crowley Lake. In June and July the fishing can be wide open. Trout key on the damselflies as they migrate to weeds and other structure to hatch. They swim in an undulating, side-to-side action, which is why I feel the Olive Woolly Bugger is so effective, the pulsating of the marabou tail simulates the swimming action of the nymph.

The most effective way to fish the subsurface emergence is with a sink-tip line, it's best to work around weed beds and retrieve the fly in short strips. During the months of June and July it is not uncommon to have 20 to 30 fish days.

The adult is best identified by its slim blue body and the double set of wings that fold over the body when the insect is at rest. This differs from the dragonfly whose wings lay outstretched when at rest. The damsel adult is not as important to trout as the nymph. It is rare to find trout actively feeding on the adults but as with everything there are exceptions.

Terrestrials

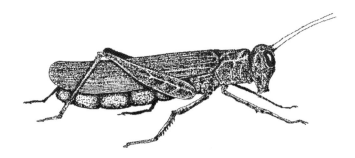

Summertime trout food, these insects really come into play in summer and early fall. Terrestrials are hoppers, crickets, beetles and ants. When the warm summer afternoon breeze starts to blow across the Sierra meadows you know its hopper time. In early summer, the hopper nymphs emerge from the warm soil and their active, jumping and feeding activity often has them ending up in the water. Once there they become trout food. When you observe this activity it is time to knot on your favorite hopper pattern and work the banks. Using a dry line and casting to the opposite bank you want to slap the fly on the surface of the water. Let the fly rest a second and give it a quick jerk. Do this three or four times to simulate a struggling grasshopper, it will provide vicious strikes if you happen to do this over a bank feeder keyed on the hoppers. If you get no activity, pick the fly up and work your way upriver casting the bank.

A size 10 Dave's Hopper will usually do the trick.

Crickets and beetles work on a lesser scale because they are usually seen in a shorter time span. In the Mammoth area this is usually the month of September. Dave's Cricket and the Black Deer Hair Beetle in size 10 are the most popular patterns.

Carpenter ants can usually be found along the streamside around old logs and timber. Early in the season the winged adult male and queen ant begin their search for territory to form new colonies. Stiff afternoon breezes blow the ants into the water where they become an easy meal for opportunistic trout. A good floating pattern such as the McMurry Ant or a black deer hair pattern works well when these airborne ants are soaring.

Spring
(April to June)

Trout season in the Sierra traditionally opens the last weekend of April, but for the fly fisher conditions are usually not ideal. Sparse hatches, runoff snow melt and sometimes even frozen lakes greet the angler. Every year you tell yourself that next season you will wait for better conditions, then as the season opener draws closer you get the urge to scratch the itch you developed during the long fishless winter. By the time the opener rolls around you're ready to be fitted for a straight jacket. There is a point where patience ceases to be a virtue.

May is a tough time for the fly fisher. Cold temperatures and blowing wind can make it miserable for the float tuber, frozen fingertips and ice-clogged eyes on your fly rod are usually what greet you in the morning. The first thought that runs through your mind is "Isn't this how I finished the season?" Streams and rivers are rushing with snowpack runoff, the consistent hatches have not started to come off yet, water is cold and the fish are lethargic, the only hatches are the midge and *baetis*. Dry fly fishing is limited. Nymph and streamer fishing is the only effective way to fish the chilled water. Fish in the streams are holding fast to the undercut banks and behind any structure that slows the velocity of the current.

Fishing in lakes requires sinking fly lines and weighted flies. The basin lakes do not usually ice-out until the middle of May or sometimes later, depending on the snowpack. The road to Devil's Postpile is closed and only accessible by snowmobile.

Fishing Hot Creek in early spring can be a crowded affair. The cold water conditions of the other waters concentrate many anglers to Hot Creek, especially on the weekends. Caddis hatches don't start until late May but there is a sparse hatch of midges and blue-winged olives for the dry fly fisher. Nymph fishing on the bottom with a split shot and indicator is also effective. San Juan Worms, leeches and Woolly Buggers stripped across the current will produce fish for nonpurist types.

Fishing on Crowley Lake can be brutal. Along with the cold water temperatures the angler can expect a stiff, cold breeze that can create white caps on the lake. This makes it exciting if you are on one side of the bay and need to paddle to the opposite shoreline to your car. The fish are usually scattered around the lake but they travel in pods. This especially holds true for the Kamloops, they can be found cruising the Green Banks area, just a few feet off the shoreline. Around June midges start to hatch in large numbers and pods of trout can be seen working them on the surface. You see so many trout it can drive you batty. You can fish them with a small caddis or mosquito pattern. There are so many insects on the water that if you want to fish with a dry it takes patience and persistence. It's tough fishing but it is possible.

Summer
(July to August)

Summer is the kindest time of the season for the fly fisher. It brings warm weather, long days and the best of all abundant hatches. The smell of pine is in the air and the rivers have slowed to gentle fishable flows. The weeds have started to form in the lakes bringing the damsels, *Callibaetis* and scuds. Warmer water stirs feeding activity in the trout the slick water surfaces become dimpled with the rings of rising trout.

By now the road to Devil's Postpile is open and all ice has cleared from the basin lakes. Backcountry trails and lakes are starting to open and backpacking anglers begin stalking golden trout. The larger species of mayflies are starting to emerge and the little yellow stonefly is hatching on the Owens. Longer days mean a brighter sun in the afternoon, most of the productive fishing time is in early morning and late afternoon.

Mammoth basin lakes in the summer months produce consistent fishing for the float tuber, damselflies are abundant and the trout are keyed in on them. *Callibaetis* are also hatching in weed beds along the shore and an Adams works well if you want to dry fly fish.

The San Joaquin River gets red hot during summer months with some wide open dry fly fishing. A small Royal Wulff or Humpy floated into pocket water or an eddy will get the attention of fish. Some days it is not uncommon for a fly fisher to have 30-plus fish days.

At this time of year Hot Creek produces a good afternoon and evening caddis hatch, size 16 caddis imitations dead drifted work well at this time. Nymph fishing is also productive when fished right on the bottom with a strike indicator.

Fish in the Owens River at this time of year can get picky. The lack of streamside vegetation works against the angler. In afternoon the sun casts your shadow across the water if the wrong approach is used, spooking the fish. You must also use stealth when approaching the river so the vibrations of your footsteps don't scatter the fish. Long leaders and long accurate casts are required if you want to fish dries. The Long Ears section of upper Owens has a good mayfly and caddis hatch, with a sporadic hatch of little yellow stoneflies.

These are the best months for fishing Crowley Lake. The weed beds are thick concentrating the fish into these areas and they are easily spotted as they cruise in and out of the weeds ambushing perch minnows, damselflies and nymphs. Matukas work well stripped along the weed channels with a sink-tip line. The Sacramento perch is also very active at this time, some days so active they make it hard for the fly fisher to get the fly down to the trout and they become a downright nuisance.

Terrestrial fishing comes into its own in the late summer months. Warm summer breezes blowing across the Owens Valley pushes an occasional hopper into the river. Hoppers, beetles, crickets and ants are found in and around Mammoth area waters in July, August and into September. Dave's Hopper, a black Deer Hair Beetle, Dave's Cricket and a black ant imitation, such as the McMurry or Carpenter Ant, work well.

Fall
(September to October)

Trees turning colors, shorter days, cooler temperatures and aggressive, spawn-ready trout await the fly angler in fall. This is the time all wildlife begin moving: Flights of ducks move in to the lakes on their way south, deer begin their trek down from the mountains to the lower elevations but most importantly for the fly fisher, the trout begin the run from the lakes into the rivers. Trout become more aggressive and take on their bright spawning colors. Afternoons become shorter as the low angle of the sun ducks behind the mountains.

Early fall still provides us with some reliable hatches. As the weather cools so do the hatches, the larger mayflies are replaced with tricos. For the most part as we progress into fall you find the best fishing is with wets, nymphs and streamers.

The weather at this time of year becomes unpredictable; you can have warm, almost summer-like conditions one day and blowing snow the next. In late October it is critical to keep a close eye on the weather, particularly if you are planning backcountry traveling. A quick-moving snowstorm can make things interesting if you are caught in the wrong place unprepared.

As I mentioned there are still some hatches going on but fall is streamer time. Hot Creek hatches are reduced to small tricos and provide sport to those who like size 22 flies in 12 foot 7X leaders. Fishing on the upper Owens gets quite good once the trout move from Crowley into the river, this usually does not happen until the late part of the season.

Mammoth basin lakes kick out some beautiful trout at this time of year. They don't produce the summertime numbers but they make up for this in quality. Brookies are brightly colored and aggressive and browns are there for anyone willing to be on the lake at the crack of dawn. Unlike the summer months when all the basin lakes are good, the fall fishing gets sporadic. You have to move around, one day the lower Twin might be good, the next day nothing.

Fall brings out the diehards on Crowley Lake. The later in the season, the more diehard the angler. The conditions can get downright miserable at times with freezing rain, wind induced whitecaps and snow flurries. I call this he-man fishing. In the last part of October you must be willing to put up with the extreme elements for a shot at the big fish and that is only if they are there. Big browns mill in the mouth of the streams that flow into Crowley and trout fatten up on the small rainbows that the Fish and Game plants in July hoping for spring holdovers.

It is not surprising to find 80 tubers fishing the Green Banks area on a fall weekend. They know that in spite of the harsh conditions these waning days of the season provide them with a lifetime of memories.

Part Four: Parting Thoughts
Catch and Release

Little by little we are seeing more quality waters converted to limited take and angling restrictions. This is a welcome sight to most of us though it seems we are not getting protection quick enough. With the increasing number of waters coming under special regulations it is important to learn the proper methods to release trout without inflicting injury. Most fly fishers practice catch and release even on waters that do not require it. It always bothers me to watch a bait fisher release a fish by sticking a pair of pliers down its gullet and ripping out the treble hooks. I've also seen a few fly fishers lay fish on the streamside to take a picture of the trout next to their fly-rod; this may make for an artistic shot, and though you are going to release the fish after the picture, all you are practicing is catch-exe-cute-release. Laying the fish in streamside vegetation removes the fish slime, their protective coating that helps to fight bacterial infections. Also make sure your landing net has a soft cotton bag, nylon and other abrasive materials are harmful to the fish.

Always use barbless hooks and try not to work the fish to the point of exhaustion, play and release them as quickly as you can. Once landed, handle the fish as little as possible and keep it in the water. Most of the time it is possible to release fish without touching it, slide your hand down the leader, grab the fly and twist it.

If you have to remove a fish from the water be gentle, remember a fish out of water is suffocating. Imagine yourself sitting down to dinner, you take a bite out of your juicy steak and suddenly a hook digs into your jaw as you are tugged struggling across the kitchen floor. As you fight against the tension, pulled through the kitchen window and landing underwater you twist and fight, gasping for air as you are held there while a huge hand reaches into your mouth to remove the hook. A dramatic scenario but nonetheless close to what a trout goes through.

Once unhooked take care in reviving an exhausted fish, sometimes after a long battle the fish may lose consciousness and float belly up. Hold the fish by the tail and gently cradle it in the palm of your other hand while *slowly* working it back and forth in the water, this will force water through its gills giving the fish artificial respiration. Once revived and it appears the fish can swim normally, release it.

Catch and release fishing not only protects a fragile ecology. It assures the protection of our wild stocks and alleviates us of the need to depend on genetically weaker hatchery fish. It is up to us to protect our resource so that future generations will have a quality fishery. It is our responsibility as anglers to practice effective catch and release methods to keep our protected waters as viable fisheries.

Wild Trout vs. Hatchery Trout

Things are changing. There seems to be an interest in the Fish and Game to move away from the old practice of relying on trout stocks to provide viable fisheries. Now instead of dumping hatchery fish into otherwise barren waters they are surveying the water to decide what is needed to support a trout population.

Our reliance on the hatchery system allows bad things to happen to our watersheds, such as water diversions and pollution. Dumping hatchery fish into the system covers up evidence of the decline of wild stocks.

The turning point for Californians was the inception of the wild trout program in the seventies. First implemented in the state's most fertile waters, the program proved to be such a huge success the Fish and Game Commission legislated that every year twenty-five miles of river, and at least one lake, is managed as wild trout water.

Often when you introduce hatchery trout into a system, you also introduce hatchery problems, such as Whirling disease. Along with the disease we also introduce a genetically inferior fish to compete with the wild stocks, these fish come from an environment lacking predators and other natural threats.

On the other hand wild trout come from an environment where only the strong survive. In the real world, Mother Nature has a way of eliminating the weak and sick, allowing only the strong, smart and cunning to pass their genes to the next generation. Not only do hatchery trout compete with wild trout for habitat, they interbreed and weaken the gene pool.

However, without hatcheries most Sierra waters would be without trout. There are also many important studies done in hatcheries that advance our knowledge of the species.

There will always be a need for put-and-take fishing. There are anglers out there who don't really give a damn where their trout come from, all they care about is a full stringer. There is room for both schools of thought.

When used wisely, hatcheries can be useful tools in fishery management.

As we run along in our busy life trying to make a decent living we tend to become preoccupied and unaware of our surroundings, unfortunately some people carry this over to their angling. The precious few hours of fishing we squeeze out of our short journey on this earth should not be regrettable. One part of being a good fly fisher is to know how to treat and deal with your fellow angler.

Unfortunately the rising popularity of fly fishing does not allow us the elbow room we had in the past. Don't crowd. If an angler is in your favorite pool, pass it by, you can return later. Think about yourself, you wouldn't want someone crowding into your pool.

When you pass another angler fishing, always give a wide berth. Stay far enough away so as not to cast a shadow across the water or vibrate the bank with heavy footsteps, trout like to hang out along undercut banks and heavy footsteps announce your presence. There can never be too much distance between you and other anglers.

When you pass another angler on the trail, smile and be courteous. If you are having a successful day and the angler asks how you are doing, be honest and helpful. Take the time to pass on useful information to the novice. We have no room for snobs in this sport.

Never jump in front of another angler, if you see they are working their way through a run, bypass them and find an area far enough away as not to crowd. Practice exaggerated courtesy.

Don't ever fish private waters without getting permission. Also, it is important to close all gates behind you, this is especially important in the Mammoth area. Many dirt roads cross gated Bureau of Land Management-leased grazing land. A few inconsiderate anglers make all of us look bad.

Remember you can't go into your local fly shop and purchase good manners along with your waders.and fly rod. You have to learn and practice them.

The renaissance the sport of fly-fishing has been going through in recent years has brought increased pressure on our fragile resource. Not only do we have to be concerned about environmental issues, such as pollution, drought and water diversions but now some of our waters are being loved to death. On the bright side, the influx of fly anglers into the sport has given us more clout. It is the nature of fly fishers to become concerned about the waters they frequent and they are quick to donate time and money. It is not uncommon to belong to three or four different conservation organizations at the same time.

The Eastern Sierra-Mammoth area has benefited greatly in the past few years due to the diligent efforts from groups such as Cal Trout, Trout Unlimited and the Mammoth Flyrodders. These groups along with others have fought and won battles for the protection of waters such as the Owens River, Crowley Lake, Rush Creek and the East Walker. Without people like this keeping a close eye on our waters it is frightening to think of the damage our fisheries could be suffering.

Another bright light in Mammoth's future is the Mammoth Lakes Sport Fishing Committee, this group was recently formed by the Chamber of Commerce to bring a better focus on the world-class fishery that Mammoth offers. It is their goal to protect the fishing environment and improve the quality and selection of the fishing available. With the committee still in its early stages of formation the jury is out on how wide it will benefit the fishery but with the joining together of fishing professionals, private citizens and business operators the results should prove positive. Another plus is that the U.S. Forest Service and the Department of Fish and Game may find a partner in protecting the area's fishing environment.

Along with these positive signs we must not forget our responsibility as anglers, conservation starts with us. Always practice sensible fishing restrictions. Even if fishing limits allow you five or ten fish a day, if you must keep some never take more than you can use. Always leave the area cleaner than you found it. Most importantly we must pass on our love and respect for the outdoors to our younger generations. Help set the foundation stones that will build and maintain a strong fishery for the future.